I REMEMBER HORSEBUNS

Rafe Mair

PROMONTORY
PRESS

I Remember Horsebuns

Promontory Press
www.promontorypress.com

ISBN 978-1-987857-25-2

Typeset by One Owl Creative in 14pt Minion Pro
Cover design by Marla Thompson of Edge of Water Design

Printed in Canada
0987654321

DEDICATION

To my children, Ken, dad to four grandchildren, Cindy with two, Karen with two, plus my first great grandchild, and to our beloved Shawn whom we so tragically lost when she was just seventeen but left her beautiful poetry to remind us that she's never really left.

I REMEMBER HORSEBUNS

TABLE OF CONTENTS

FOREWORD

by Grace McCarthy

If you love British Columbia, you will find yourself captivated by Rafe Mair's sensitive reflection of growing up in Vancouver. This portrayal of his life and times is when Vancouver itself was growing up. Rafe's life was shaped by the times that his parents knew: the Great Depression, World War I, and World War II. Sometimes serious, sometimes humorous, this book describes a good life, and one gets the feeling while reading it that the author is having a very good time recalling the people, places, and times of the era.

I first came to know Rafe Mair in 1975. We were in the Cabinet of the Government of British Columbia under the leadership of Bill Bennett. Bill was an outstanding Premier and had an ability to keep the strong group of individuals elected within that year together and working as a team. We found ourselves in the midst of a severe recession and the challenges were many. Rafe was a hard worker and fit immediately into the government work, which included the 7:00 a.m. cabinet meetings (Premier Bill Bennett's idea) in Victoria. I can look back on those days and remember that Rafe worked very hard in the important responsibilities he was asked to oversee.

After his political career, Rafe's interest turned to broadcasting, and his *Open Line* show with its huge audience heard Rafe give his opinion on the news of the day. It was required listening for all politicians because Rafe, once exposed to being in government, couldn't resist straightening out the politicians both in Ottawa and Victoria.

I have not always agreed on some of Rafe's spoken or written opinions. I suspect he has not agreed with me during the times we worked together forty years ago. Now, a few differences of opinion over forty years has not weakened our shared respect and friendship. It is an honour to know Rafe and his family and to introduce Rafe's story. It is safe to say Rafe was no stranger to controversy, his listeners had strong views as well and some disagreed with him and some agreed, but it all made for interesting *Open Line* radio. Rafe's life and Rafe's voice has made a difference in our world.

As you finish reading this book, you will be moved to remember the youngster who played in the forests, enjoyed fishing with his Dad and his friends, explored the streams and rivers, and began a lifelong love of the precious nature and the glorious mountains of British Columbia and the people who touched his life.

I especially enjoyed Rafe's anecdotes of his dogs. They were obviously treated well, and took on human personalities in the book. People who love animals are the best! If they are blessed with a great sense of humour, even better!!

It is to be expected that Rafe's early years growing up in Vancouver would morph into a deep appreciation for this wonderful land in which we live. His attempts to help bring awareness to how we treat this space have been a deep and steadfast commitment to the people and to the province, and for that he has invested years of his time.

Rafe, thank you for inviting me to write these comments on this book. How fortunate we are to live in British Columbia and to have been given the opportunity to serve our country, our province and our city.

Grace M. McCarthy,
O.C., O.B.C., LL.D., D. TECH., F.R.A.I.C. (Hon.)

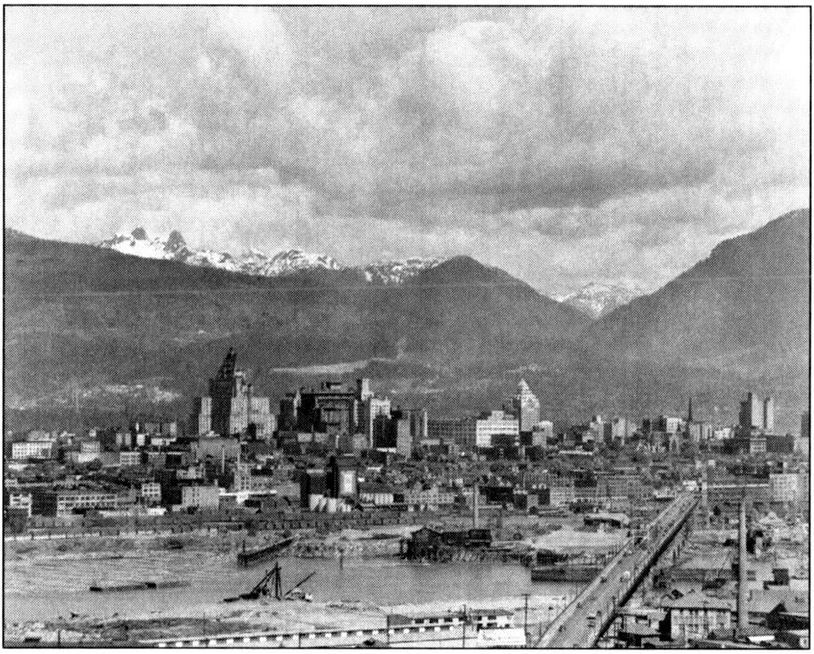

Vancouver 1948.

I was in grade XI and thought I lived in a huge city!

Photo courtesy of the City of Vancouver Archives, photographer Jack Lindsay

INTRODUCTION

All those writers who write about their childhood! Gentle God, if I wrote about mine you wouldn't sit in the same room with me.

– Dorothy Parker

I don't think anybody should write his autobiography until after he's dead.

– Samuel Goldwyn

This is a book of personal thoughts, recollections, and opinions. In past books, I've spoken about my life at various stages but at this point, having exceeded my Biblical span by a decade plus, I want to look back on a very happy and fortunate childhood that morphed into an interesting life, and the impact my upbringing and surroundings had on me and what I did.

Mostly this is a book about my beloved city, Vancouver, and my land, British Columbia, and how they have affected my life. I must confess from the start that I am a British Columbian through and through and that this is my main allegiance. No longer having to worry about votes or ratings I think I can spell that out!

Many years ago when I was on radio a caller asked me if I was a Canadian or a British Columbian first. I unhesitatingly replied "British Columbian" and I expected callers to crap on me from a great height, but I was surprised that the response was quite favourable.

I think there are a number of reasons for my prejudice. I have absolutely no family connection in any other region of Canada with one exception—my six-generations Canadian goes back to an early Clanranald Macdonald, a refugee from the early nineteenth-century Highland Clearances, who took his family to Nova Scotia. My maternal grandmother, whom you will meet, was Jane Macdonald, born and raised in Cape Breton Island, who spoke Gaelic before she spoke English. As a Nova Scotian she had about as much love for central Canada as native British Columbians do.

In school I was taught about Canada as if it were history of Ontario dealing with Quebec, a perpetual nuisance, thrown in. I couldn't relate to the people or the places. All of the First Nations tribes I learned about were from that area and, to my great long-term regret, I learned nothing about BC First Nations even though there are more of them than in the rest of the country combined. There are even more individual First Nations languages in British Columbia than in the rest of Canada combined.

Even as a child I resented this Central Canada bias. I was ornery very early in life! Interestingly, I learned from Grand Chief

Edward John that he couldn't understand a word spoken by his neighbouring tribe but could understood the Navajo in Arizona. Would that we learned that sort of thing and gained an earlier and better understanding of our own fellow citizens!

I frankly found Canadian history boring as hell especially when I compared it to the people who spawned, fought, and perpetuated the American Revolution. This did not make me pro American—it was just so damned interesting because of all the philosophical debates behind the revolution, the causes of it, its uniqueness in world history, the reasons for it, and the consequences. No fights for liberty in Canada were fought because devout monarchists did not think fighting for liberty was necessary. There were no fights for a new form of government because no one seemed to want one.

In reading the biographies of Adams père et fils, Jefferson, Madison, Benjamin Franklin, Patrick Henry, John Marshall, and many others, I was, plainly, inspired. George Washington, not a great general, was a very great leader and without him, victory could not have happened and, more importantly, the new federation would not have survived its first decade. Sir John A. Macdonald, on the other hand, appeared to me to be a tiresome old Scottish immigrant who drank too much and got into local politics and fought with George Brown who was probably the most boring politician ever created in this country, and that covers a lot of ground.

I'm unable to think of any great Canadian political philosopher or inspired revolutionary with a cause. If Macdonald or any other founding father wrote anything that was not only inspiring but actually inspired anyone I'm not aware of it. I can think of no Canadian who was a leader of Washington's importance, a political philosopher to match a Franklin, Madison, or Jefferson. I can't think of a practical and brilliant politician to match Alexander Hamilton, either. Hamilton is a fascinating study. Born and raised in The West Indies, and an aide to George Washington in the war, Hamilton became the financial guru of the new republic who, as a Federalist, supported a strong central government—as did Washington—putting him in a perpetual conflict with Thomas Jefferson, a Republican (in the terminology of that day) believing in "States Rights".

This lack of comparison is no doubt due to a number of factors but is no less true for that. If you are of a revolutionary bent, and I am, you will find your inspiration in France and America and, ironically, from some of the best philosophers in the UK, even though it mostly kept its revolutions under wraps through incremental concessions by the "establishment".

America didn't fulfill its political promise from the start. It sanctified slavery at the beginning and failed to really end it with the Civil War. America produced Abraham Lincoln, the greatest man of the last 200 years, but couldn't put his principles into practice. It will be interesting in generations to come to see the impact of the election of Barack Obama. The US conquests of its territory were cruel, brutal, and racist. Its people are warlike by nature. They are prone to violence. I don't want to live there and never have.

But as a kid, as today, I was a history buff and a lover of biographies, and I gravitated toward what I found interesting. I simply was not inspired by Canadian history or those involved nor did I find it nearly as interesting as American history.

We are what we are and we can't remake history even though that's what the "we know best" crowd try to do. Sir Isaac Brock was not a Canadian and the War of 1812 was not a Canadian war no matter what the "higher purpose persons", in Denny Boyd's marvellous phrase, in Ottawa tell us. Canada was not created on great principles, valiantly fought for by men of great bravery and bold ideals, but in a series of negotiations for commercial reasons and to provide a traditional British shelter against American absorption made more probable by the end of their Civil War. BC's entry into Canada was scarcely a love match but an "arranged marriage".

In any event, I am a Canadian because that's the way it worked out and, far from wanting to see the country go badly, would like to reform its system (I've been writing and speaking about that for many years) and achieve unity, so that we all really do have equality from coast-to-coast and all feel part of the same nation.

I owe it to readers to tell them where I'm coming from so there can be no doubt.

This is a book of recollections, many from childhood, and the consequences. I haven't spent a lot of time on the Internet because that's not the point. Anyone can find out what happened historically; it's quite another thing to recall what happened to you as you grew up, what influenced you, what you loved, what you didn't, and what you most remember. It is this that I've tried to accomplish.

My love for my beautiful city and province continues, not unabated, but much increased as old age captures me. I now live on Howe Sound, the soul of the Lower Mainland, in lovely Lions Bay, and am much involved in local environmental matters.

This, then, is a love story. I hope, perhaps, you will at least see this effort as the curate saw his egg—parts of it are excellent.

PROLOGUE

I have been commissioned to write an autobiography and I would be grateful to any of your readers who could tell me what I was doing between 1960 and 1974.
– Jeffrey Bernard (who was drunk most of the time!)

In Vancouver, during the '30s and '40s and indeed into the early '50s, things like bread, eggs, and milk were delivered from door to door by a deliveryman in a horse and wagon. In fact, if there was snow, the horse drew a sled. This meant that the streets were covered with horse buns. This didn't seem to cause anybody any angst; we were considerably less fastidious then. In fact, in those wartime days of "Victory Gardens", horse buns came in very handy. One can only imagine what a fuss a sudden harvest of street apples would cause to the general public today!

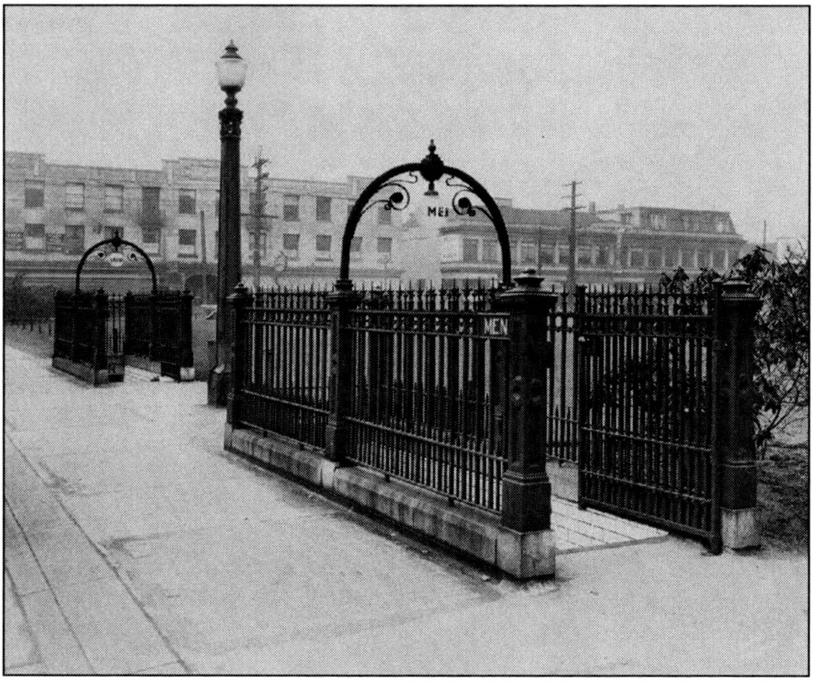

Comfort Stations, Robson Street.

People were better served than horses.

Photo courtesy of the City of Vancouver Archives, photographer W. J. Moore

Speaking of horse buns, our neighbours' dog, a nasty little Scottie, used to poop on our front lawn, which annoyed the hell out of my father, especially when he was mowing the lawn. His answer was not to call the authorities but to try to train Mandy, our gentle Spaniel, to return the favour!

I have special memories of our milkman who, at Christmas, taking the odd libation from friendly neighbours, was always eight sheets to the wind when he reached our house and was never known to quite finish his route even though the horse did!

Just before I leave home food delivery, I must mention the "Chinaman", a term we used back then to describe our deliveryman who, in his ancient model T truck, used to deliver fruit and vegetables door to door. Our deliveryman was a delightful fellow, of indeterminate age, named Low Yo, who delighted in sending me in some dates, which I loved, whenever I was home with one of the usual childhood diseases. My mother, from a generation where Chinese men were cooks—her family had one—used to speak to Low Yo in her own brand of Pigeon English, which he had no chance of understanding but took it all in good humour.

Now, let's get on with it.

MY HOME AND NATIVE LAND

Patriotism is the last refuge of a scoundrel. – Samuel Johnson

After the 1992 Charlottetown Accord, which I fought tooth and nail, failed to pass, well known writer Peter C. Newman wrote me and said my gloating—I deny it ... well, maybe a little—had offended him, one of 30 percent of British Columbians who had voted "Yes".

I wrote him immediately! "How dare you call yourself a British Columbian! BC Citizenship is like a Scottish Clan—you must be born into it!"

One can become a British Columbian second class but in Newman's case the Committee hadn't finished its preliminary review and I was forced to tell him that the outlook wasn't all that great though he did have in his favour the fact that he wasn't actually born in Ontario.

Former Premier Mike Harcourt once said—on air would you believe!—that he was a British Columbian whereas on making enquiries I learned that he didn't arrive in BC until he was six weeks old. "Too late—must be born here," I replied.

Now we're fair. By an earlier ruling the committee has pronounced former Speaker of The House of Commons John Fraser a full citizen, for while he was born in Yokohama, his father, a British Columbian, was working there at the time.

Canadians from most parts of the country, especially Atlantic Canada, become British Columbians second class after an informal canvass of their background. (The committee is considering making all Macdonalds from Cape Breton Island automatic British Columbians but some grumpy losers have raised the issue of my grandmother and the matter is in limbo.)

It is, I must say, much more difficult nigh unto impossible for someone from Ontario to accomplish this. Especially those from Toronto. I thought it might help Ontarians if I outlined one or two positions they must freely take as preliminaries. Unless they do so, their applications are non-starters.

They must, from head down to the wiggies, despise the Toronto Maple Leafs. It must give them almost insufferable pleasure when they miss the play-offs (again). Even when Toronto Maple Leaf players are traded, they're not to be trusted. Ditto the Toronto Blue Jays and whatever their basketball team is.

Many years ago, when my stepchildren were about seven and nine respectively, the Toronto Maple Leafs played an exhibition game against a Czechoslovakia team. My wife made it clear that as a Canadian father I would have to cheer for the Canadian team. I grumpily agreed and at about the two-minute mark Czechoslovakia scored and I was heard throughout the neighbourhood cheering, "Yes!"

I was once asked what my dearest sports wish was. I answered, "It's the bottom of the ninth, two out, the deciding game of the World Series with Toronto leading my beloved Dodgers 25-0. There is a scratch single, a bungled infield play, and a dropped ball in the outfield, and to cut to the chase, the Dodgers win 26-25 and the entire City of Toronto walks en masse into Lake Ontario."

It's critical always to remember that the rag's name is really *The* Toronto *Globe and Mail* and must be called that on all occasions. Any legislation or policy approved of in, or even suggested by anyone from Ontario is, ipso facto, not in the interests of British Columbia and must be rejected vigorously. British Columbia is *not* part of "The West". We are, in the name of Jean Barman's wonderful book, *The West Beyond The West*. Any backsliding can call for second-class citizenship being stripped away with no right of appeal. Reading either the so-called *Vancouver Sun* or *Vancouver Province* (save, of course, *Dr. Morgan* or *Luann* in the comics) is discouraged. The onus is upon the reader to prove he or she was reading the comics only.

Every convert from other areas must send letters to at least five people and one newspaper in their native home, in February, telling about the weather, enclosing colour photos of the Japanese Cherry blossoms preferably in the Stanley Park Causeway along with shots of daffodils from the back garden.

I'm sure that Ontarians will recognize the generosity of these rules.

BORN TO THE VILLAGE BY THE SEA

I must down to the seas again, for the call of the running tide
Is a wild call and a clear call that may not be denied;
And all I ask is a windy day with the white clouds flying,
And the flung spray and the blown spume, and the sea-gulls crying.
– John Masefield

I was born in Grace Hospital, the Salvation Army hospital, in Vancouver, on 31 December 1931 to Kenneth Frederick Robert Mair, a native of New Zealand, born on 29 July 1906, who arrived in Vancouver with his parents and two sisters from Auckland in 1913, and Frances Tyne Leigh, born in Vancouver on 8 November 1906.

On 31 December 1931, Conservative Richard Bedford Bennett was the Prime Minister of Canada. Another Conservative, Simon Fraser Tolmie, was premier of BC. James Ramsay MacDonald was prime minister of the UK, George V was the monarch, Dr. Heinrich Brüning was Chancellor of Germany, and Herbert Clark Hoover was President of the United States. Benito Mussolini, "the Duce", was fascist leader of Italy. Winston Churchill was in "the wilderness years" and Hitler was becoming more and more a factor in German politics. Franklin Roosevelt was Governor of New York.

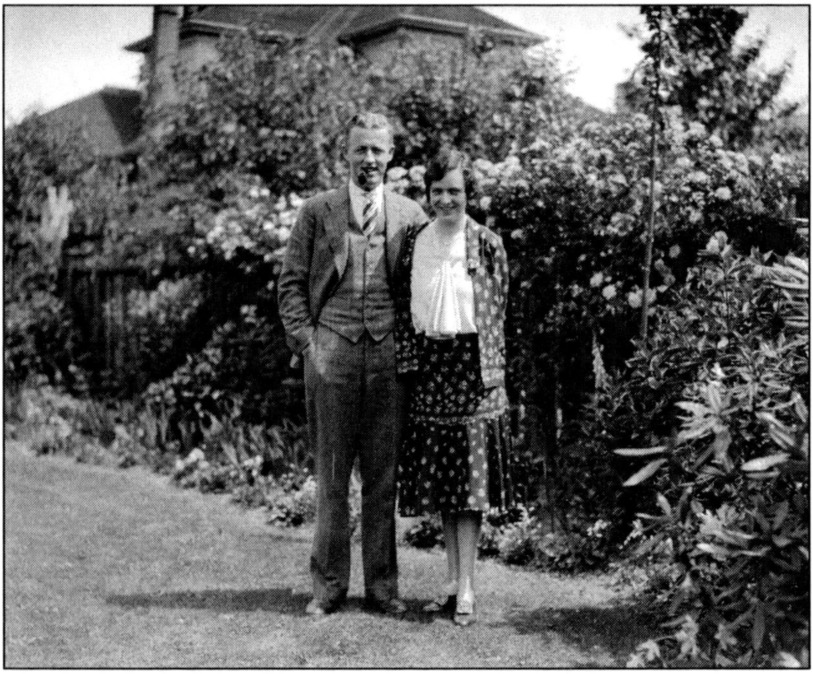

Mom and Dad's engagement picture, Point Grey, 1930, published in the Province.

Both my parents grew up in the West End of Vancouver, which in those days was "the" place to live. I don't know how they met although there must have been many opportunities. My mother often mentioned a former fiancé, Steven, whose memory was invoked by the playing of Hoagy Carmichael's "Stardust", surely one of the loveliest songs ever written. I always thought that Mom carried a torch for Steven but she never told me what happened to the romance.

My parents were married at St Paul's Church, in the West End and very much still there, on 8 September 1930, by The Right Reverend Canon Harold King. I was christened by Canon King early in 1932 at St Paul's. I was born, then, on the "right side of the tracks", meaning the west side of the city, and had a privileged upbringing in a middle-class family that provided me with an excellent education including four years at a private school during the Second World War. I graduated in Law from the University of British Columbia in 1956. I was born into the "establishment", which loosely meant those who had established themselves in "better" neighbourhoods and were better off financially than those who lived elsewhere—and were British, by God!

I had mostly a kind, loving upbringing but on two matters I carry a grudge to this day. I was never permitted to wear what the other kids wore and in fact it was a struggle to get my first long pants by Grade IX. Going to school and indeed everywhere in short pants, when all your contemporaries have long ones, is a humiliation not easily forgotten. Wearing draped slacks when they were all the rage was out of the question. Secondly, by the time I was thirteen my face was covered with peach fuzz, which caused great embarrassment. Somehow I was considered too young to shave. Finally, my mom relented and permitted me to shave the moustache and when I did, I said the hell with it and shaved the lot. For some reason my parents, especially my Dad, didn't want me to grow up. The embarrassment this caused made life much easier for my kids, especially Ken, who inherited his old man's early facial hair.

As I got older, I came to resent my position in the "establishment". Whether that was because I felt uncomfortable being privileged from birth and not by accomplishment, or whether I lacked confidence that I could compete with my confrères, is an open question.

Vancouver, then as now, was divided into the "east side" and "west side". The "crossover" was minimal and structured. We played soccer and rugby against one another and those of us on the "west side" often worked in East Vancouver—American Can at the foot of Heatley St was popular—when we were going to university. I made lots of friends from the East Side, many of whom I met later in life, and many of those have done very well indeed. Most, however, succeeded without the luck of birth that I had and perhaps are stronger for that. I believe there is more contact between the two solitudes now. It is amazing how physically similar the various districts and neighbourhoods are today, to what they were, including the ethnicity of the residents.

As mentioned, my mom was born here in 1906 and her mom, my beloved Gram, came here as a young lass from Cape Breton Island. She was Jane Macdonald (small "d" please) and she married my Gandi, Leonard Leigh, from Minnesota, in Vancouver.

Gandi was from an ancient and well connected English family. Some years ago, there was a biography written of detective storywriter, Dorothy L. Sayers, a kinswoman, which confirmed our relationship with the Spencer family, thus Princess Diana and the Churchills. We also claim descent from the Drake family of Devon, though not directly from the great mariner himself since he had no children. My great great uncle, Sir Percival Leigh, was the editor of *Punch* magazine and has his name carved in the famous "round table", still to be seen at the Punch Tavern on Fleet Street.

Even being several generations removed from the Highlands, Gram was a Scot who spoke Gaelic as well as beautiful English. She went to her grave claiming that she had never met a Campbell she liked or trusted and wouldn't dream of having Campbell Soup in the house! For those curious about this, Google "Massacre at Glencoe" and you'll have your answer.

The Mairs were a pioneer European family from Aberdeenshire that settled in Paihia in the Bay of Islands, New Zealand, in the early 1800s, the first being my great great grandfather Gilbert Mair who, along with my great grandfather Robert Mair, helped found Whangerei, the largest city north of Auckland, the latter donating the land that is now Mair Park. One of its districts is Mairtown; there is Mair Street, and Deveron Street named after the river they lived by in Scotland.

Dad and his family also lived in the West End. His parents were Leslie Mair, son of Robert, from Auckland, and Blanche Coates from Salisbury, England. He had two sisters, his twin Lois ("Lo") and younger, Bertha ("Boo"). Dad was tall and very fair, and Lo was very dark and short. In fact, Lo looked quite Polynesian, as did her daughter Ann and, to a lesser extent, my daughter Shawn. This led to the theory that the family had Maori blood but as much as I would like to, I can't trace it. Two of my great uncles had Maori wives and from one, William, is descended a present day well known Maori activist, Ken Mair. Curiously, my father, myself, my son, and my eldest grandson all have Kenneth as our first name. When I show my passport to NZ immigration officers it always commands quite a laugh!

Mom went to Crofton House, a school started and run by the Misses Gordons. It was then located in the West End and the "better families" sent their daughters there. I'm not sure what that made Dad, who attended King George High School, which used to be on the southeast corner of Burrard and Nelson. One of his classmates was Mary Livingstone, comedian Jack Benny's wife, who was a part of his show. Mom had two younger siblings, Leonard and Peggy.

Both my dad and my mom, like most kids they knew, were taught to swim by Joe Fortes, the famous Afro-American who taught at English Bay and who is now immortalized, if that's the right word, by a posh restaurant in his name on Thurlow near Robson.

Also growing up in Vancouver at that time were the parents of many of the kids I grew up and went to school with—I think particularly of the Owens, and especially David and "Pip", the latter as Philip becoming Mayor of the city and a damned good one. Dad's friend, Walter Owen, later a prominent lawyer and

Lieutenant-Governor of BC, was always "Uncle" Walter to me. My dad and mom were "Uncle" Ken and "Auntie" Frankie to the Owen kids as Mayor Philip Owen reminded us all at my "Roast" in 2000. Daughter Margaret Owen married classmate and well-known tax lawyer, Jacques Barbeau, and Daphne married businessman Michael Francis, and they are good friends of Wendy and me.

Mom's family's summer home was at Spanish Banks. Gram and the kids would take the streetcar to Broadway and Granville—the end of the line—and the "man" would pick them up in a horse and wagon for the long and tedious journey to the cottage. Gandi would take his putt-putt across English Bay and join them on the weekend.

My dad's parents, Leslie and Blanche (called Phyl), Pop and Nan-Nan as named by my older cousin Ann Hatfield, had their summer place at Grantham's Landing on what is now known as the Sunshine Coast. It was there that my Dad, as a boy, started his lifelong love of the ocean and salmon fishing, loves he passed on in spades to me.

By the time I was born, my parents had moved to Point Grey. About all I can remember about it was our dog, a lovely and loving English Sheepdog named Skipper. It's not surprising I remember Skipper since, according to mom, he never let me out of his sight.

I do vaguely remember Nanny, who on one occasion, took me to St James Anglican Church in Vancouver East to see their Nativity scene. Nanny was evidently very religious and I remember her reading me Bible stories, most of which scared the liver out of me. I have no recollection of when or why she left.

Our next home, of which I have a clearer memory, was on Quesnel Drive. I remember looking out the kitchen window in the morning and waving goodbye to Dad as he drove down the steep hill to work. I recall the inconsequential like the leaded windows, the window boxes with Nasturtiums, and the day the police came into the neighbourhood to arrest a teenager who had stolen a car.

Our next home was at 43rd and Macdonald. There was the sawdust man who let me ride in his truck, the postman who took me home to Mom after catching me stuffing the mailbox with letters I had "written", the time I took my little hatchet and chopped a lot of shingles off the side of the house, and when, after seeing Mom prune some flowers, I proceeded to cut off every bud in the garden. Mom was horrified but later said that she had never had a prettier garden. There my best friend was Gregor MacIntosh, whose grandfather was former BC premier, Sir Richard McBride.

We then moved to 6390 McCleery St, which was just north of Southwest Marine Drive; I think it was the beginning of 1936. My memory here blurs into memories of the house across the street at 6389, which Dad had built in 1938 and where we stayed until 1948, by which time I was in high school. We lived on McCleery St when I went to Jack and Jill Kindergarten, Maple Grove Elementary, St George's and the first year plus at Prince of Wales High School. It was McCleery St, 6300 block, where I spent most of my formative years. It was at 6390 my brother Leigh arrived in November 1936 with a nurse named Miss Howell, which I thought an apt name for a nurse to this screaming addition to the family.

My part of Vancouver was down and dirty racist. Not violently so, but racist as hell. There was a "Chinatown", a "Japtown", a district where Jews lived near Marpole delicately called "Kikeville", an area where Italians lived, and so on. Racism was overt in the British European community, and while not vicious, very real. It was pure segregation. The Chinese were called "Chinks", the Japanese "Japs", the Jews "Kikes", and all Indo Canadians were called "Hindus", even though most were actually Sikhs. The "proper" establishment didn't even like Roman Catholics very much—they were called "Micks" and "Dogans"—and in fact my uncle and Godfather, Bill Hatfield, (married to Lo, with children Ann and Barbara) whom I very much looked up to, a prominent doctor, who'd never in living memory darkened the door of the church except to get married, had a hissy fit when his elder daughter, Ann, decided to marry a Roman Catholic. The marriage took place anyway and lasted until the groom died some fifty years later. It was a very happy marriage and my cousin Ann, whom I saw as my "big sister", and her wonderful husband Clark were very close friends of mine until he died in his early seventies and she in 2013. My parents had no such animus against Catholics, and Bill and Lo came to love Clark as if he were their own son.

During World War II, the Italian community felt caught in a bind. Was it loyal to the "old country", which was allied with Nazi Germany, or the Allies? A young lawyer named Angelo Branca read the riot act to the community and their loyalty to the Allied cause thereafter was never in doubt. Branca went on to be one of the best-known criminal lawyers in the country and ended his career as a justice on the British Columbia Court of Appeal. I had the honour of appearing before Branca, J. several times. An amusing story: Dad had a young Italian lad named Mario working for him and when, in September 1943, Italy changed sides and joined the Allies, Mario wailed, "I can't figure out if I'm just a poor dumb 'Wop' or a 'glorious ally'!"

The Downtown I remember had three "skyscrapers". The Marine Building, which easily out-did the old Hotel Vancouver, and the new one, opened in 1939 just in time for the visit of the King and Queen. My early memory of the new hotel was getting caught in the revolving front door and being scared as hell. I have never liked revolving doors since. Across the street from the "new" hotel, then as now, was Christ Church Cathedral. There were lots of small apartment blocks and houses all along Georgia to the west of Burrard.

The old Vancouver Hotel was where Sears, soon to be Nordstrom, now is, and was famous after the war as homeless returned-servicemen squatted there. Other buildings, the Medical-Dental, the Devonshire and Georgia Hotels, were there as now, as was the Rattenbury-designed Courthouse, now the Vancouver Art Gallery. Francis Rattenbury, an Englishman, designed the Parliament Buildings, the Empress Hotel, the old Hotel Vancouver, and countless public buildings, including courthouses all over BC. I pled cases in the ones in Kamloops, Vernon, and Vancouver, the latter of which is now the Art Gallery. Rattenbury returned to England in 1929, and in 1935 was murdered by the chauffeur, the second Mrs. Rattenbury's lover. This was made into a play by Terence Rattigan called *Cause Célèbre*, which I saw, starring Glynis Johns, some years ago. Francis's son John [Rats], who was at St George's when I was, became a prominent architect in Los Angeles.

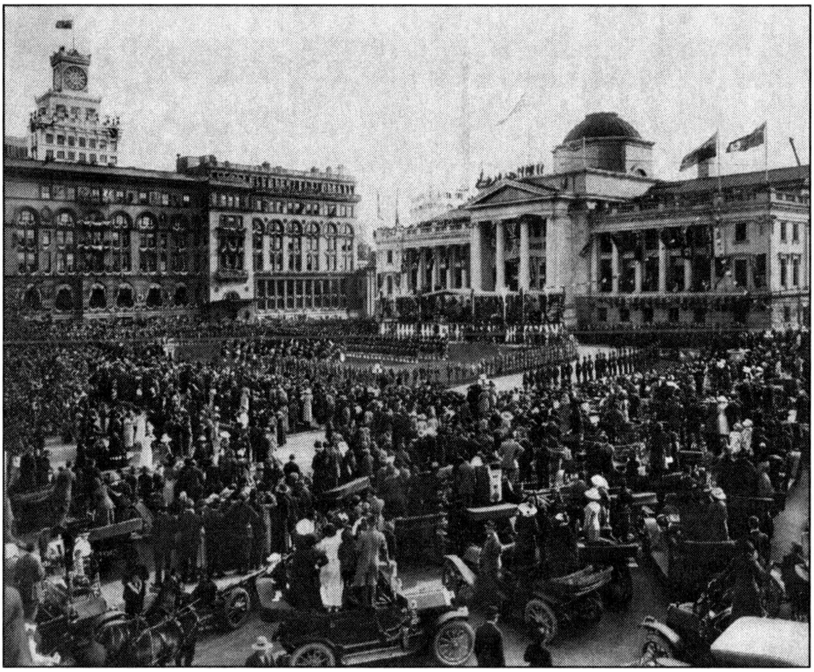

Old Courthouse, now Art Gallery, 1919.

Thank God we haven't messed with this one - yet.

The Medical-Dental Building was where Dr. Campbell (settle down, Gram), my first dentist, worked. I hated him—there was no freezing and he worked the drill by foot peddle and I thought he seemed amused at my discomfort. Perhaps he knew of my Macdonald ancestry!

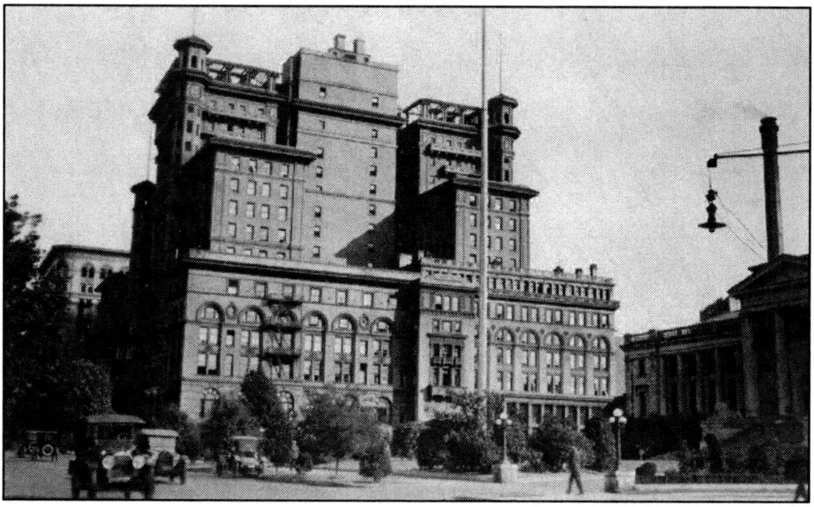

Old Hotel Vancouver.

We got rid of this for the Eatons/Sears/Nordstoms building.

Photo courtesy of the City of Vancouver Archives

A big thrill for kids was going to the Sylvia Hotel on English Bay in the West End—very much still there—to "Dine In The Sky" on the eighth floor, which gave a view of the downtown and the North Shore mountains. Today that's hard to believe as apartments block the view of everything except the next building! The Sylvia is still there and does, of course, still have a brilliant view of English Bay and beyond. Across the street over English Bay was a roller rink, now long gone, and that's where we Sea Cadets trained in the war. (English Bay was by my time no longer fashionable for swimming; Spanish Banks, Locarno, and "Kits"—Kitsilano—were "in".)

Transit was by streetcar in the city and interurban from

Vancouver to Richmond and New Westminster. As kids, we would take the interurban to Richmond and Eddy's Nurseries where we would make twenty-five cents an hour weeding—I have never voluntarily weeded since. If you lived near a stop, the interurban was a quick hop to downtown Vancouver. Public transit was owned by the BC Electric Railway Company, later taken over by WAC Bennett in the fifties to become BC Hydro and Power Authority. The interurban tracks are still there and the dream of reviving the system lingers on. The right-of-way is now part of a great struggle between the City of Vancouver and the CPR, which owns the land, complicated by nearby residents who, as squatters on the right-of-way, have built gardens. There's now also an effort to bring the streetcars back, which in my view should never have been replaced in the fifties by buses, a view shared by many experts in the field.

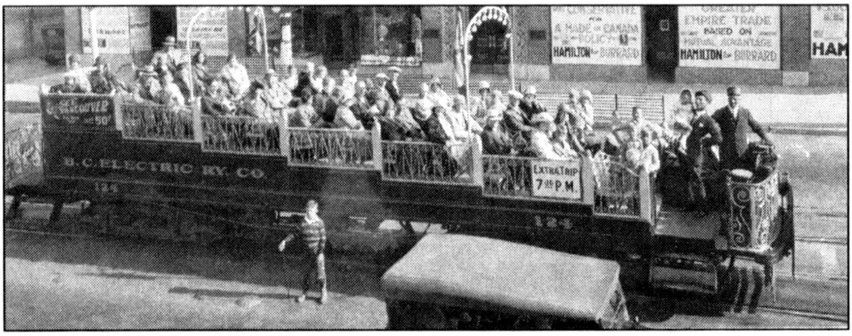

Teddy Lyons and his observation car.

Loved by kids. Dig the pants on the kid in the foreground!

Photo courtesy of the City of Vancouver Archives, photographer Harry Bullen

I recall with vividness the open streetcar where Teddy Lyons would entertain, through his megaphone, the tourists aboard and the passers-by. He was famous for his corny jokes. Like all kids, I was sure that Teddy was looking right at me.

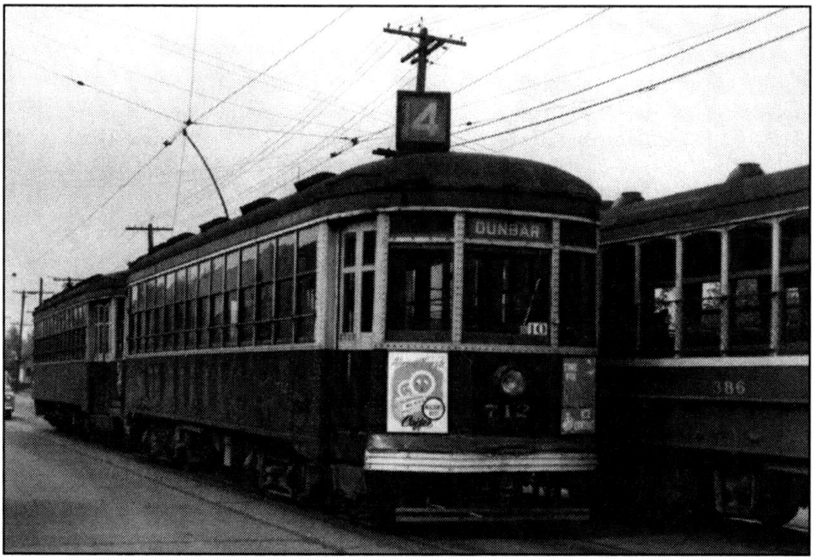

BC Electric Street car.

Woe that we ever replaced them with buses!

Photo courtesy of the City of Vancouver Archives

Our streetcar from downtown to our stop at Macdonald and W41st was the number 8, which terminated at 41st and Dunbar. The Dunbar streetcar, which completed my journey to 29th, and St. George's School starting in 1942, was number 7. Both were double cars and for some reason kids all took the rear one. In those days, it would never even occur to us not to stand up at all times for a lady of any age and an older man if it was crowded. Kids got eight tickets for a quarter, and adults got four.

At 41st and Dunbar there was a neat bakery that sold delicious glazed doughnuts, three for a dime, and it was next to Nightingale's Drug Store, which had a candy counter and a magazine stand, with comic books, out of Mr. Nightingale's sight for easy pinching.

HOWE SOUND AND NORTH WOODLANDS

The sea, once it casts its spell, holds one in its net of wonder forever.
– Jacques Yves Cousteau

Don't grow up too quickly, lest you forget how much you love the beach
– Michelle Held

Howe Sound, for thousands of years the home of the Shíshálh and Squamish Nations, was "discovered" by George Vancouver in 1793 and named after Admiral Lord Howe. It is BC's most southern fjord and one of the most beautiful—and, properly treated, one of the most bountiful.

BC is a grand place for a child who loves the outdoors to grow up. I mentioned that my Pop and Nan-Nan had a cottage at Grantham's Landing. This overstates the case—it was more like a shack. Funny little memories. The shack had, naturally, an outdoor privy and since my aim was not very good, and hasn't much improved with time, the edge of the "hole" was sometimes (well, nearly always) sprinkled with drops of urine, and I remember Mom asking me if I could sit down to piddle, raising for the first time the geographical misunderstanding of women generally on this matter.

When I was a little boy, my parents would take me to Grantham's Landing for the summer. Mom and I would go up in May on the Union Steamship *SS Capilano*, and when we went home in September, the captain would let me sleep in his cabin, a great thrill. Dad commuted and, amazingly, I remember the day in 1935 when I was three, when he arrived and told us that "Pier D" had burned down. This was a CPR pier and it was a very big deal indeed. Amazing what a child remembers!

I remember being stung by a bee and my aunt Peggy, my Mom's sister who was only twelve years older than I, with the help of some boy friends in the battle to hold me down, putting "bluing" (a wash day substance) on the wound. I really have no idea why "bluing" was supposed to help but it ranked right up there with castor oil, cod liver oil, and iodine pills, as remedies for whatever ailed you. I got even with one of the lads shortly thereafter when I grabbed some tickets to a dance from his hand, tore them up and threw them into the ocean. Wasn't I a nice little blighter?

Grantham's Landing hasn't really changed all that much. I still remember so well looking across the bay at the beautiful green lawn on Keats Island—it's still there today. I remember the beach where I built myself a little raft and used to paddle under the careful eye of my mom. I have fished that beach with a fly rod for sea run cutthroat many times since and the whole area really hasn't changed, may the Saints be praised, very much.

I started my fishing "career" at Grantham's with shiners off the local dock. I spent hours, head down, forelock in the water, carefully seeking out these little fish with a hand line, small hook, and bit of mussel or sea worm, and catching them by the dozens. I can only hope that in the hereafter there aren't thousands of vengeful little fish waiting to get even!

My shiner fishing continued at North Woodlands, and the most amazing shiner fisherman I ever saw was my uncle Bill Hatfield's black Labrador bitch named Darky. That would not likely be a suitable name today! Darky used to sit down at the wharf and gaze into the water, wait patiently, then all of a sudden scoop with her mouth and bring up a shiner, and throw it onto the dock. It was not unusual to come down to the dock and find Darky sitting next to a dozen dead shiners!

Grantham's Landing, then and now, a beauty spot on the Sunshine Coast, was a marvellous place to fish. Dad had a putt-putt with an Evinrude outboard, which used to drive him nuts! It had a little nob on the top—no rope—and one spun the nob and prayed that the engine would start. It often took longer than my father had patience. I have a recollection of looking at the top after the engine was running and it appeared as if there were two tops. I didn't understand why this was so and in fact don't yet!

When I was twelve, Dad gave me a small Evinrude outboard for my dinghy along with a crescent wrench, which he told me was for changing the spark plug and hitting the "goddam engine" with when it wouldn't start! It served both purposes very usefully. This started my lifelong dislike of engines.

In those days, salmon were so plentiful that in order to get "skunked" you would have to forget to put on a spoon! Dad and Mom fished for salmon with cane rods and large wooden Peetz reels—I still have one—using a large Gibbs-Stewart "Diamond" or "Tom Mack" spoon. I, on the other hand, had a hand line with a small Tom Mack, as my quarry was grilse, or as we wrongly called them, salmon trout. They were in fact immature Coho salmon. Once I accidentally hooked a Coho on my hand line. The line streaking through my hands burned the hell out of them. I landed the beast to the great pride of my parents to say nothing of my own. My reward was being allowed to use a rod and reel thereafter.

There were lots of places to fish close to Grantham's—I think of Gower Point, Gospel Rock (so named because of the Bible verses painted on it), Salmon Rock on Keats Island, and Big and Little Popham Islands. Not far from the Pophams was Hermit Island, which the Hatfield's shared with the Reginald Tuppers, he being a well-known Vancouver lawyer later famous for chairing a Commission into corruption in the Vancouver Police Department. It was his coverage of this hearing that first brought the famous open-liner Jack Webster to public attention.

Hermit Island was a wonderful place for kids to roam and it actually had a hermit who made neat ginger beer. On the west side was a huge cliff called Battleship Rock because it looked like that when the waves broke on it. David Tupper, son of the neighbours, was a teenager with a .22 rifle, which scared the hell out of my auntie Lo! I next saw David many, many years later when he was Treasurer (President) of the BC Law Society, a post his father had once filled. His grandfather, Sir Charles Tupper, was a Founder of Confederation.

Cousin Ann was my big sister and hero and remained so for the rest of her life. She was the "responsible" one and always got "responsible" jobs such as rowing the Queen Mary, a large rowboat, and being the only child allowed to do so. Somehow I had no childlike resentment of this authority—though resentment of authority was a lifetime trait—such was my hero worship.

Pop and Nan-Nan were often at Hermit and Pop would play streetcar with us on an old log. He played a banjo and often sang "risqué" Maori songs to us. Nan-Nan would remonstrate, saying, "Leslie—don't you know these are young children you're singing to?" Nan-Nan didn't seem to understand that our knowledge of Maori was extremely limited! I especially liked "Kitipura", evidently about a lady whose morals didn't impress Nan-Nan.

Uncle Howard, Hugh's dad, his Mom being Auntie "Boo", Dad's younger sister, was often there and played with us a lot. Somehow the adults didn't care too much for Howard Bardon but we kids thought he was wonderful. He played with us by the hour and always had candies for us, a very good start. Howard's problem was that he was veddy English, tall, thin, handsome, and broke. He was a remittance man whose remittance always seemed to be late. When the war came, Uncle Howard was suddenly in his element.

In 1942, the Hatfields sold Hermit Island and bought another island on Indian Arm of Burrard Inlet at North Woodlands, owned for years by the well-known Tepoorten family. On the charts as Lone Rock, it was simply called the "Island" by the family, and I spent what seemed like a wonderful decade there as a teenager—of course in all likelihood it was more like five or six years.

My two Hatfield cousins grew into very comely lasses indeed. Ann, being older, attracted boys like flies to molasses. I wanted to be part of the "big kids", not Barbara's "little kids", and therefore became very interested in their music. This interest in jazz and swing lasted the rest of my life and I'll tell you a bit about it later.

I fished all day, every day. I used to fish off the east side of the "Island" at a place suitably called Cod Rock. (My quarry were wrongly called "cod" but were really Pacific Rockfish). I'd catch shiners off the dock, put them in a bucket of water to keep them alive, then use them live at Cod Rock for "cod". Then I'd skin and fillet the cod, sell the meat, and use the heads for bait for the crab net. I developed a pretty neat little business amongst the people at Woodlands selling them fresh cod and crab.

One time I didn't have any bait for the crab trap so, at Uncle Bill's suggestion, I got a small sack full of clams, smashed them in the sack, tied it inside the crab trap, and used it for bait. I put the trap down not far from the dock and the next day when I arrived at the dock and looked out, there was a very large Lingcod moseying around it. I very quickly caught a shiner, and with it on a slender shiner line, threw it out to the Ling. He took the bait and with considerable difficulty I landed him. In fact I was afraid that the shiner line would break, so played him as if he was a salmon! Uncle Bill came down, weighed it, and it topped the scales at ten pounds. A pretty substantial bonus for somebody who was just going to check a crab trap! I was a hero with Bob, Kenny, and Hugh, though that didn't last.

Usually my cousin Hugh was my fishing partner and Bob Hutchinson and the late Kenny Ward from South Woodlands would often join us or we would meet them at Grey Rocks and fish near their place. A few years ago I was at a reunion party at South Woodlands and, for the hell of it, suggested to Bob that we catch some shiners and go get us a cod or two, as in former times. Bob told me, "Rafe, the shiners are all gone and so are the cod." Bob married my first sweetheart, the lovely Diana (Dinny) Fraser, who remains beautiful.

One day in 1943, dad took me over to Snug Cove on Bowen Island, and bought a fifteen-foot sailboat, which he named the *Sindbad,* and I learned to sail. He was very particular about the spelling, saying that was the way it is spelled in *1001 Arabian Nights.* It was a wonderful experience enhanced the following year when dad bought a Snipe, a registered fifteen-and-a-half footer with Egyptian cotton sails.

In 1944, I went sailing with two companions alongside another sailboat, a tiny one-sailer called a Penguin. We ran into a squall, the Penguin then tipped over, and we lowered our sails and waited for help. Eventually help came in the form of Auntie Lo, who rowed the *Queen Mary* out to rescue the Penguin, and the proprietor of the store, Percy Squires, came out to get us in his putt-putt. Bearing in mind that this was wartime, amazingly enough the story made the front page of the *News Herald* a couple of days later complete with a picture of Auntie Lo entitled "plucky mother".

A sailboat was quite an attraction for young ladies. There was an attractive girl living in South Woodlands who was a couple of years older than me and I had the hots for her. I took her sailing and we crossed the inlet and landed at Jug Island. One thing led to another and we began to neck. I boldly placed my right hand on her left boob and she went ballistic. She screamed at me that I should never do that to a girl! Advice I persistently ignored for the rest of my life. It did, however, make the sail home a little bit awkward. I wasn't sure if she was still mad at me or if she had changed her mind.

I became a lifetime lover of sailing although I really didn't get to do much until later in life when Wendy and I sailed several boats, the last being a beautiful Cal 29.

North Woodlands was served by the only boat named an official Post Office in the British Empire. *The Scenic,* a very odd-looking former tug, that chugged along at about six knots, was the main source of supplies and transport of people to and from the communities it served. It was owned by Northland Navigation, which also owned *The Harbour Princess* that ran daily from Vancouver to Wigwam Inn at Indian River at the top of the North Arm.

The Scenic was skippered by—are you ready for this?—Capt. Andy, who was a delightful old codger who used to allow us to get on the boat at the North Woodlands wharf and then, as it went past the "Island", let us dive off and swim to that wharf. Any number of rules and regulations today would forbid such fun.

We did have another small supply boat, a strange red boat of perhaps 30' called the *Seabiscuit*, which was from the nearby Quarry, in Deep Cove.

I should mention that the water in the North Arm is very cold compared to that in Vancouver and Howe Sound; I don't know why. It also, unlike them, has red jellyfish that sting like hell. One learned to be careful!

FYSHINGE WITH A FLIE

They say you forget your troubles on a trout stream, but that's not quite it. What happens is that you begin to see where your troubles fit into the grand scheme of things, and suddenly they're just not such a big deal anymore.

– John Gierach

Give a man a fish and he will eat for a day … Teach a man to fish and he will sit in a boat and drink beer all day …

My fishing took a different turn in 1942 when my father and mother took me to Lac Lejeune near Kamloops. We traveled with Meredith ("Med") and Nancy ("Nance") McFarlane; "Uncle" Med being a very prominent lawyer and one of my heroes.

It was a time of wartime gas rationing so we all went in one car, which was interesting with four adults and two car sick kids. Going over the then very scary Fraser Canyon Highway, all gravel with huge drops to the Fraser River, we had a leak in our gas tank. With rationing, this presented a problem. Not to worry! The adults chewed gum, using it to block the hole until we could get to a service station in Ashcroft Manor.

This was to be my first look at fly-fishing. Dad had shown me his packet of flies and I was enthralled. They were tied in the English manner by an Englishman named Bill Nation, a well-known guide in Kamloops who also guided, in the off season, at Lake Taupo in New Zealand, later my stomping ground. Nation's flies were considered to be the cat's ass until the '60s, when more BC-oriented patterns were pioneered by people like Jim Kilburn and Jack Shaw of Kamloops. Until then, Nation's Sedge, Nation's Special, Nation's Red, and so on were de rigeur. In any event, looking at Nation's flies must've stuck because in years to come I loved to tie them even though I no longer used them.

I wasn't allowed to cast a line because my mother was afraid I would lose an eye so I was restricted to trolling a fly, which pissed me off and stoked my desire to fish as the adults did. My first cast came "illegally" one night when I was supposed to be babysitting my little brother while the adults had dinner at the lodge. I went down to the dock with rod and reel and surreptitiously cast a fly, clumsily and not far, and hooked a very small but very welcome trout. (These were "Kamloops Trout", which genetically are Rainbows). I had to tell my Dad and rather than giving me hell, he seemed a bit proud, as I certainly was. I was bitten by the bug and the habit became life-long.

One day we went to Black Pines Lake. The walk seemed endless but probably was an hour or less. "Auntie" Nance kept us going by getting us to sing songs like "This old man, he played one, / He played knick-knack on my drum, / With a knick-knack paddywack / Give a dog a bone, / This old man came rolling home" and "I know a man / Named Michael Finnegan, / He grew whiskers on his chinnigan, / Along came the wind / And blew them innigan, / Poor old Michael Finnegan." Great fun!

My dad caught a beautiful fish at Black Pines as we both fished from a sunken rowboat (by this time, wearing dark glasses, I was allowed to cast). "Uncle" Med cleaned Dad's fish, wrapped them thoroughly in newspapers, and set them on fire. The fish was delicious! I've never seen or heard of a fish cooked that way since. This was a great initiation to fishing with a fly and many years later when I moved to Kamloops, I fished a great deal at Lac Lejeune.

As I grew up, it was Meredith "Med" McFarlane, QC, who instilled in me a love of the law. I read Blackstone's Commentaries, Great British Trials, and the lives of great barristers like Edward Carson, Marshall Hall, and F.E. Smith, courtesy of "Uncle" Med. Years later I had the honour to appear in front of him in The BC Supreme Court and The BC Court Of Appeal. (By way of amusing aside, I had three appeals with him sitting as one of the three judges, won them all, with him dissenting in all three!)

THE FISH WIN

All the romance of trout fishing exists in the mind of the angler and is in no way shared by the fish.

– Harold F. Blaisdell, The Philosophical Fisherman

While in my teens and early twenties, my father would take me on his yacht, *The Gleniffer*, over to Flat Tops near Nanaimo and we would "strip cast" with herring for Coho. One day I also caught a thirty-three-pound "Spring" or "Chinook" salmon.

Those were the days! You could hardly avoid getting your limit and I guess that was the trouble—too many of us did just that for the good of conservation.

Out of my boyhood in God's Country came a strong love of fishing, but as the years have passed I've become a wuss—not yet a full-fledged wuss but a hell of a lot closer than I ever thought I would be.

It all started about twenty years ago when, as a very keen fly-fisher, and dedicated fly tier, I started to have problems killing fish. Then the great fly-fisher and author, the late Lee Wulff, came out for "catch and release" and that solved my ethical problems—except it didn't, for then I read an article in a British fly-tying magazine by a man I admired enormously, Hugh Falkus, now sadly departed. He minced no words in saying that "catch and release" was unethical for it tormented animals for human pleasure. If you want to fish, said Falkus, keep what you're going to eat then quit. No ifs, ands, or buts.

Bullshit! I didn't take to this notion. Fish couldn't really feel the hook could they? Of course not—weren't they cold blooded? For whatever the temperature of your blood means. But they struggled. Oh, how they struggled! They sure as hell weren't having any fun! But did it truly hurt? Surely not!

Then, in February 2007, Wendy and I were fishing our favourite river, the Tauranga-Taupo, on the North Island of New Zealand at Lake Taupo. I was landing a nice five-pound hen Rainbow when, as I drew her to the beach, I saw three others of a similar size swimming up with her. Goddammit! Don't tell me they fucking well care! They don't have any familial feelings do they? I'd seen this happen many times before but this time, somehow, it shook me. I mean *really* shook me.

I vowed this trip was the last of my fishing days. I would give away all of my fishing library (that weren't classic first editions), and all my fly-tying stuff carefully acquired over the years, and all my tackle. I had fished from when I was a small child to a man in his seventies and, just like that, I quit.

Wendy, a damned good fly-fisherman, had her epiphany the same day, when she snagged a small fish in the eye. For her, that was happening too often and it really bothered her.

We both solemnly vowed to quit.

After a suds or two that evening, we recovered our senses and laughed at how silly we had been to think of quitting.

Then it happened. A few days later, we went to supper at a game fish club we often frequented in Mangonui and as we sipped a beer before dinner, we saw a charter vessel bring in and string up their catch, a large shark and two magnificent marlin. We watched the blood run down their sides and asked why. Why in the name of God would anyone do that?

We both quit. Thousands in redundant rods, reels, and fly-tying stuff. All gone. It wasn't easy, I can tell you. Those damn deep sea beauties did it. It wasn't just the cruelty to animals bit, although that lingered, but the absence of a justifiable—perhaps sensible is the better word—reason. Neither of us could shake the simple question: why? A question that had to apply to trout just as much as marlin.

I don't want to sound too virtuous here because my knees and general health have become so bad that perhaps my quitting could be seen as making a virtue of necessity. I have quit fishing and I miss it—a lot. And I miss tying. The saving grace, I suppose, is that I'm no longer able to fish.

WHY DO WE KILL WHEN WE DON'T HAVE TO?

If slaughterhouses had glass walls, everyone would be vegetarian.

– Paul McCartney

In the years since I stopped fishing, I've pondered the question of the relationship between man and beast and I always returned to that damned squirrel I shot as a youngster and how he lay there, balls up, and how awful I felt. I've never shot at anything again but always told myself that killing a fish was different than shooting a squirrel ... wasn't it?

In any event, I'd come to a watershed. As Yogi Berra said, "When you come to a fork in the road, take it!"

I got to know Anthony Marr, the famous animal rightist. He didn't try to convert me—he likely sensed, correctly, that my natural contrariness would take over any intelligent argument he could make. But he made me think and I started to mull over some uses we make of animals that I couldn't justify. I assessed my own hypocrisy from the start. I eat meat, wear shoes, and have a couple of beautiful Turkish Lambskin jackets. Anyone accusing me of hypocrisy has me dead to rights. I still asserted that I had a right to be heard—but what was I to say?

We've outlawed cockfighting, bear baiting, and dog fighting in our part of the world though we're haunted by Macaulay's taunt, "the puritan hates bear baiting not because of the pain it inflicts on the bear but the pleasure it gives to the spectator."

Why do hunters go after deer and moose when they could buy beefsteaks for a tenth of the cost? Okay, they do eat them, but why do men, mostly, want to kill mountain sheep and grizzly bears? Or any kind of bear for that matter. I say this knowing that I sound like the recently reformed smoker.

I went to the Bullfights in Mexico about forty years ago and nearly lost my dinner. This was rank cruelty. The bull was taunted until he got pissed off enough to go after the matador. I found myself immediately pulling for the bull. They tell me that the bullfights are losing favour—I hope so.

Why do people hunt deer with a bow and arrow when they know that their victim will suffer enormously?

Why do we kill baby seals? Because they can be usefully made into ladies' coats? Do women need these coats? Given what they pay for the seal, can't they afford something else? This, surely, is a clear case of supply chasing demand for the obvious reason that no ladies would go cold for the absence of a seal coat.

Why do we let Japan kill whales for "experimental reasons"?

Why hasn't Paul Watson been given the Order of Canada? Why does the world stand aside, Paul Watson always excepted, when Faeroe Islanders slaughter pilot whales every year just for the hell of it? No, they don't own these cetaceans that travel the oceans and they are not in any way essential to their food supply. Moreover, Faroese also kill porpoise and dolphins for no other reason than they have done so for 1,000 years. I have been to Faroe and noted that on the back of one of their bills is a depiction of a man hacking a pilot whale to death.

Why do we permit rodeos that feature cowboys riding bulls whose balls have been bound and who clearly don't care for the practice?

Many claim the right to kill things because they've always done so. It doesn't take much imagination to visualize what our society would look like if that were the criterion by which society judged itself! Some say the Bible gives us permission.

I'm not yet in either the Kingdom of Wuss or the Kingdom of God though I fear I'm far closer to the former than the latter.

CRUISING THE COAST

There is nothing more enticing, disenchanting, and enslaving than the life at sea.
– Joseph Conrad

One can be so close to a situation as to forget to notice it! Such it is with the beautiful coast of British Columbia where I was raised and familiarity has no doubt made me blasé about my great luck. I was very fortunate to have spent a lot of time on the coast as I have mentioned but I was doubly fortunate in that when I was twelve, my father bought a powerboat called the *Bradscott*. It was about forty feet long and plenty big enough for all four of us to sleep on comfortably. We took a great many overnight cruises up the coast, sometimes for as long as a week.

Just after the war my father traded in the *Bradscott* and bought the *Gleniffer*, forty-five feet overall.

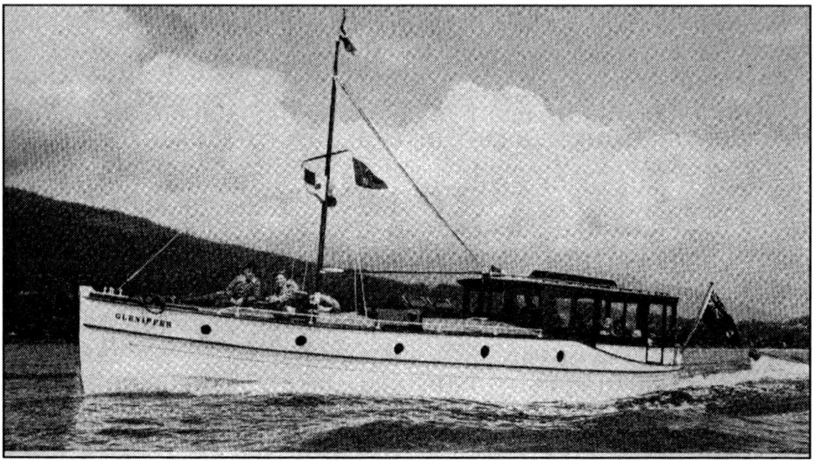

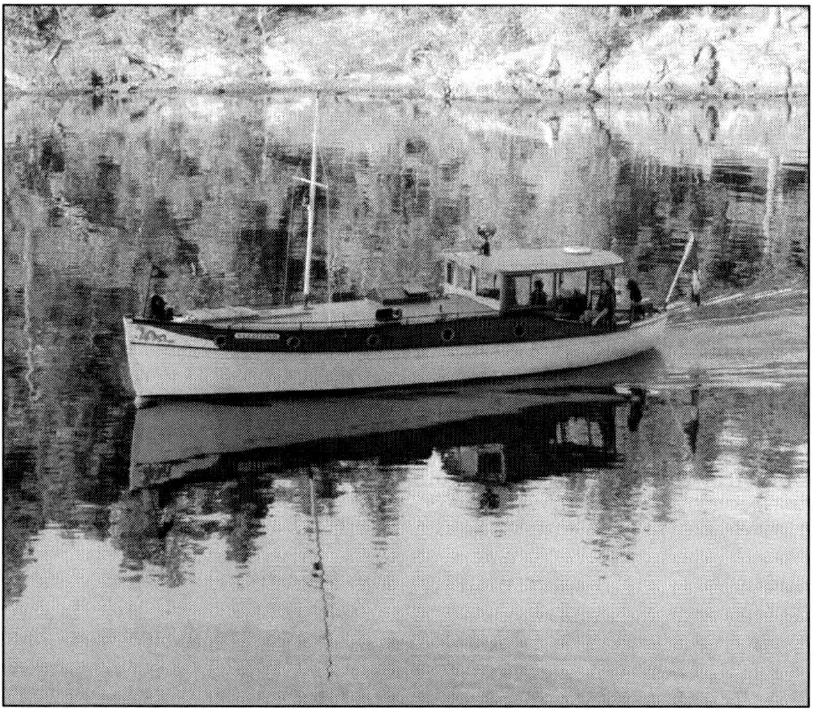

The Glennifer, built in 1912 in Hong Kong.

A grand old lady still going strong!

Photos courtesy of Tom Burnett, Salt Spring Island

The *Gleniffer* was quite a craft. It was originally a Chinese junk brought to British Columbia to be converted into a pleasure cruiser. Unhappily, the owner went broke and the junk lay at the mouth of the Fraser up on a sandbank for many years. It was rescued by a well-to-do lumberman who converted it to the power cruiser it became, and a wonderful job he did.

The *Gleniffer* was solid teak and, while by no means modern looking, was as stately as a dowager Queen and always the centre of attention. She is still around.

Dad became an instant Captain Bligh. There was a new yachting cap, with a badge of indeterminate origin, and a strange new salty nautical jargon, which we were all expected to understand. As time went on, we got a ship to shore radio, and my father became a "Sparks", hailing vessels all over the nearby ocean. He really came into his own when he became Staff Captain of the Royal Vancouver Yacht Club, which entitled him to a cap with a legitimate badge and, of course, a similar badge for his blue blazer. Nothing would do until we had a special warrant to fly the Blue Ensign, which was much like the old Canadian flag but blue. Somehow it was important and prestigious. When he received this, it was proudly flown as if the *Gleniffer* had had something to do with the thrashing of the Spanish Armada.

One of Dad's proudest moments came in 1948 when the *USS Iowa*, a sister ship of the *USS Missouri* (which had received the Japanese surrender in 1945, and was the largest warship afloat) came to Vancouver. Dad sailed the *Gleniffer* to her stern and dipped her flag as a salute, and the Iowa returned the compliment. The picture of this appeared in one of the newspapers.

An entire book could be written on just where we went over the many years we did our cruising. I remember so many different places. I must start with Howe Sound where we poked into every nook and cranny. The Gulf Islands were a great favourite and a lifetime can be spent cruising in and out of them.

Desolation Sound was a great attraction and I'm happy to say it isn't much different today than it was then. One of my favourites was Princess Louisa's Inlet, part of Jervis Inlet. When I was sixteen I worked at Malibu resort at the head of Princess Louisa and it's a part of the world that has to be seen to be believed, gloriously beautiful with the mountains jumping out of the ocean. I recall particularly the great fishing and I also will never forget swimming amongst the seals.

Savary Island, with its beautiful sandy beaches, sticks in my mind as does Thormanby with Buccaneer Bay and, near Pender Harbour, both Smuggler's and Secret Coves.

It is very difficult to give a decent word picture of the British Columbia coast at all, much less in a few words. There are the mountains rising straight out of the ocean, the grandeur of which takes of the breath away. Even after a lifetime of visiting the tall evergreens to which, at sea level, are added to the gorgeous arbutus, Canada's only native broad leaf evergreen tree, which features peeling bark and changing colours, the novelty is never gone.

The sea life is varied and always with you. There are seals, sea lions, porpoise, killer whales, other orca, and extensive birdlife capped off by the glorious baldheaded eagle.

In looking back over the geography of my childhood I can only say that I cannot imagine any place more beautiful in the world to grow up. Moreover it leaves a deep impression that shapes you in such a way that it is always part of you, and you of it, no matter where you go or how long you stay away.

I had some great times cruising with my parents in this fantastic land of ours. I have, of course, many memories. I saw a lot of the coast, and God only knows how many clams and oysters I scraped off the rocks for the old man and me to pig out on.

I recall one day when Dad sent me to get some clams. Back I came from a nearby beach with a bucketful of butter clams. Dad looked at me, looked at the bucket, and asked, "Don't you want any?" I dug another bucket and we ate the lot!

He had a great trick for getting the sand out of the clams. He would place them in a large pan, fill it with fresh water, put salt in, then sprinkle the top with rolled oats. Left for half an hour, the clams spat out all their sand. I'm damned if I know why, but it works.

I caught lots of fish including mud sharks in Long Bay, Gambier Island, the latter serving no purpose except the thrill of the hunt. I never learned to like eating salmon—catching them? You bet, but eat them? No thanks. When I was a Cabinet minister I noticed that at every luncheon I was invited to they served salmon. I went back to the office one day and complained to my secretary that I had bluddy salmon again. "Oh," she said, "they asked me what you liked for lunch and I said you always had salmon!"

What constantly amazes me, living as I do on Howe Sound,

is that with a city of over two-million people, there are so few boats. Marinas and yacht clubs crowded with vessels, but an ocean nearly bare!

SUMMER CAMP AND HOMESICK

A lot of parents pack up their troubles and send them off to summer camp.

– Raymond Duncan

In 1941, I went to summer camp at the Qualicum School For Boys. Our headmaster was a Mr. Lodge whom I met later at St George's. One of the features came at night time when the tradition was to engage in pillow fights until Mr. Lodge came in and gave two or three of the boys the slipper. Naturally this hurt but somehow didn't operate as a disincentive.

I hated most of the time there and was truly homesick. There were, however, a couple of highlights. I met a lot of boys who I knew and became good friends with later on in life. I have learned over the years that most of them were about as homesick as I was. I really was a loner. I did very well playing by myself—no! I didn't say *with* myself—and I remember pleasant hours on the huge beach, which at low tide went out for what seemed like miles. I remember using the "Sea Biscuits" as toy soldiers and capturing the small flatfish in the pools the tide left behind.

I learned to swim in a rather unusual way. There was a raft, about 100 yards off the beach, that the "bigger" boys would swim to and then dive and frolic. I couldn't go, of course, because I couldn't swim. One day, watching all the big kids having so much fun, I decided to hell with it, waded in, and simply swam to the raft, with the lads and Mr. Lodge cheering me on. It considerably enhanced my prestige—very important in a boys' camp!

This was wartime, and I remember singing wartime songs, many of which were verses of Mademoiselle of Armentières from World War One, always ending "inky, dinky, parlez-vous". The verses were usually mildly naughty, though, in those days when "hell" got you in trouble, they were thought by us to be punishably naughty.

Looking back, it was not all bad, I suppose, but I was happy as hell to go home.

While at camp and fishing with two other boys, a "Blackfish" came up alongside our small boat and scared the hell out of us. "Blackfish" is the colloquial name for a killer whale. It was huge.

Let's fast forward to the early '60s. I took my six-year-old son Ken to the Point Grey bellboy near the mouth of the Fraser River to do some fishing and we suddenly found ourselves in the midst of a large pod of killer whales. I was, of course, very concerned that Ken would be scared stiff but he obviously sensed that the whales posed no threat. All he could say to me was "mint", which was the word of the day for "fantastic". It was one of the great experiences of his life and to this day he talks about it. In his house there are a number of pictures of whales hanging on his walls. Unfortunately he has lived in Toronto now for many years but the British Columbia coast has left a lasting impression. He retains a love of fly-fishing. As he says when asked if he comes from Toronto, "I *live* in Toronto, but I'm *from* British Columbia."

Living as we do in Lions Bay on Howe Sound, we see lots of killer whales that have made a marvellous comeback in recent years, as have porpoise and larger humpback whales. At this writing, the Howe Sound communities are fighting a proposed Liquefied Natural Gas plant in Squamish in order to protect these mammals.

A SHOPPING WE WILL GO!

Whoever said money can't buy happiness simply didn't know where to go shopping.
– Bo Derek

I hate to admit it, but our family didn't really feel the Depression of the "Dirty Thirties" all that much. My father was always working, which was a big plus in those days, and for my Uncle Bill and Auntie Lois Hatfield and family, money didn't seem to be a problem. Bill had a spinster stepsister with loads of money, known as Auntie Janet. She was goofy as hell and would give Bill money from time to time when she felt like it without rhyme or reason. Mom used to tell how Auntie Janet once replaced all the rugs in the Hatfields' house on W41st and Marguerite at a huge expense "out of the blue", then gave Bill a package of cigarettes for Christmas! Evidently she gave him enough money over all that, along with what he made as a well-known physician, he did very well.

On Saturdays, Mom and I would often be picked up by Uncle Bill's big black Packard and his chauffeur, Roberts, known as "Rarsh", would drive us downtown. We all loved Rarsh but we didn't much like the Hatfields' Nanny, called Nurse, who was always so crabby. You guessed it—Rarsh and Nurse got married. I never heard of them again.

Usually Auntie Lo and cousin Ann would be along on our Saturday shopping odysseys. We would park right in front of the Hudson's Bay on Georgia, such was the absence of parking problems in those days. The "Bay" looked just as it does now. Along Georgia Street to the east was Kelly's Music, sadly now gone, where Auntie Lo would buy the contemporary music she loved so well. Often, as I got older, these records would find their way to me as birthday or Christmas presents. I was very close to my Auntie Lo and loved her dearly. And, of course, I adored cousin Ann.

Across Georgia Street was the Strand theatre, where Mom took me to my first ballet, Swan Lake, and on the corner of Georgia and Granville was Birks and the Birks clock, the place where Vancouverites met. Birks was torn down and the business moved, along with the clock, to Granville and Hastings in 1994. Just south of Birks on Granville was and still is The Vancouver Block, with its large clock on the top, where I had my first law office in 1961.

Across Granville Street from The Bay on the west side was Purdy's Chocolates, which had a very fine restaurant. We would usually go there for lunch and Mr. Forrester would give us kids gold paper-covered chocolate coins, which we loved and looked forward to as the best part. Mr. Forrester was a neat guy. He lived up the street from us and had a walnut tree and let us kids help ourselves.

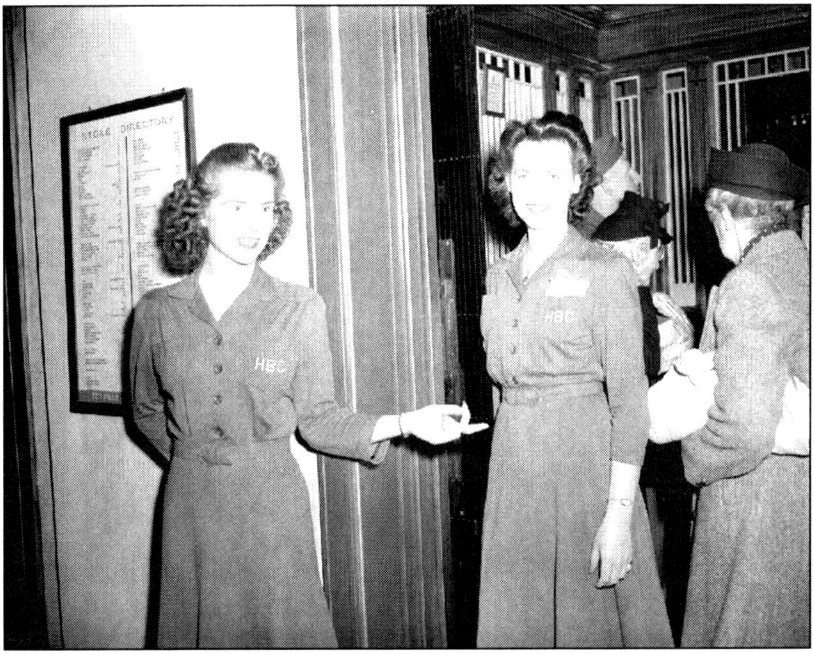

Elevator girls at the Hudson's Bay Company.

Alas, a casualty of modern times.

Photo courtesy of the City of Vancouver Archives, photographer Don Coltman, Steffens Colmer

A feature of shopping "downtown" was the street photographer who snapped your photo, gave you a receipt, and you could get the result a few days later. Most teenagers had pictures of themselves holding hands with their sweetheart. I had one of Heather and me, later autographed by Frankie Laine, which I kept long after we broke up (Heather and I, that is) whether because of the autograph or that I still carried a torch for Heather, I can't say. Probably both.

Our favourite department store was family-owned Spencer's on Hastings Street, which had the best Toyland and Santa Claus at Christmas. "Mr. Chris" Spencer would usually be in evidence and he invariably greeted customers by name. The store, unlike the more modern Bay, had wooden escalators, which our mothers warned us were very dangerous but we all used anyway. I never heard of anyone getting hurt.

In 1948, Spencer's was bought out by the Toronto-based Eaton's and my grandmother was so outraged that she forbade us ever to shop there. Being a Cape Breton Islander, Gram didn't like Toronto any more than Vancouver people did. Indeed, "old" Vancouver much resented this unwanted invasion, considering it an outrage. I must say that in later years, after Gram had departed this vale of tears, I sometimes shopped at Eaton's and almost every time I would have a bad experience. I would walk out, look up at the sky, and say, "Gram, you were right." When it went broke in 1999, I was delighted but was sad that it hurt the employees, who had been browbeaten by the company and summarily dismissed if they even mentioned the word "union", yet the Eaton family, I'm told, stayed filthy rich.

Both The Bay and Spencer's had staff choirs at Christmas that sang carols on CJOR radio where I later worked. CJOR was in the Grosvenor Hotel near Robson and Howe, torn down in 1983. Across the hall from CJOR was Blaker's Barber Shop with

Mr. Blaker, son Alf, and "Frenchie". (We boys all snickered at "Frenchie" because to us that meant a condom!) Dad or Pop would take me there on a Saturday for my haircut and I would spend spare moments nose up against CJOR's window hoping to see the "GG man" or the owner of some other familiar voice. After, we would have a bite at the nearby White Lunch, so-called because, in its earlier days, only "whites" were welcome.

It's worth it, I think, to hear the story of this restaurant chain for it fortifies what I said earlier about Vancouver's racism:

A number of White Lunch restaurants operated in the city. Other locations included 865 Granville, 737 West Pender, and 714 West Pender.

The White Lunch name reflected a policy of serving and hiring only white people. The civic government of the 1930s reinforced racism in the culinary industry by passing a 1937 ordinance that prohibited white women from working in Chinatown. Whites believed they had a properly appointed place in the Darwinist order and needed to protect white women from "lascivious Orientals." A delegation of 16 waitresses from 3 restaurants marched to City Hall on September 24, 1937 to protest the ordinance but the mayor refused them a hearing. Restaurant proprietors had their licenses revoked if they failed to observe the civic ruling.

In 1939, white women were allowed to work in Chinese-owned restaurants that served only "English meals to English customers." When Vancouver's white society recognized China as an enemy and victim of the aggressor and an ally of democracy in WWII, racism against Chinese residents began to dissipate ...

– Courtesy of AHA Media

Woodward's Department store was also on Hastings Street and it, too, was a favourite BC company with other stores around the province. It went out of business in 1993. One of its features was a beacon on the roof, which shone a revolving light all night long and, as I remember, it was shut down during the war so as not to show Japanese bombers where to bomb us.

Woodward's stores were popular outside of Vancouver and I think particularly of Kamloops. Charles "Chunky" Woodward was the owner of The Douglas Lake Ranch near Merritt and there was a scarcely a horse person in the area that didn't have the opportunity to ride there and to get involved in the competitions he put on it. He was very popular and his untimely death much mourned.

Then, as now, the Army & Navy was situated between Hastings and Cordova, and was popular for those seeking a bargain, especially in fishing tackle. "Army & Navy for value, we always sell for less" ran the radio jingle. Nearby on Cordova was Harkley and Haywood's tackle shop, very up market, which unhappily bit the dust in the Recession of the 1980s. Its fishing man, Colley Peacock, was a famous fly-fisher right up to my early days living in Kamloops. As a child I watched in wonderment as a lady tied flies for the store, a hobby I picked up big time in later years.

On Granville opposite The Bay on the west side were a couple of shops that I remember, including butcher James Inglis Reid,

("We Hae Meat Ye Can Eat"), sadly no more, and Ingledew's Shoes, pretty much where it is now. On the east side was Sweet Sixteen, a clothing store for younger women, and Saba Brothers, a high-end ladies clothes store, both gone.

Clarence Saba of Saba Brothers was a friend of my family's and often came to our cocktail parties. He was, Dad would confide to any who listened, not Jewish but Lebanese. To that generation of West Side Wasps, this was apparently of critical importance. When I went to Prince of Wales High School in 1946, I dated a girl named Janet Jabour. My Dad informed me that, thank God, Sam Jabour, Janet's father, was Lebanese and not Jewish. This was typical of the times when anti-Semitism was virulent and worldwide, not just in Germany.

Along the east side of Granville, south of The Bay, were the theatres there today, the Capitol, the Orpheum and, built during the war, the Vogue. Across and down the street to the north was the Lyric where mom took me, when I was about eight, to see the famous Shakespearean actor, Maurice Evans, in *A Midsummer Night's Dream*. Directly across the street from the Orpheum were the Plaza and Paradise. The Lyric, Plaza, and Paradise all died when TV was born. I remember Mom taking me to the ballet at the Orpheum and I especially remember *The Nutcracker* one Christmastime.

Saturday was the day we kids would go downtown to a movie—when we became teenagers more to neck than watch the movie! Across from the downtown theatres was the Silk Hat restaurant that, amazing for those wartime days of sugar rationing, served soft ice cream, often as part of a fruit salad. It cost a quarter and was all the rage.

Just south of the Silk Hat was a used record shop where you could get yesterday's hits for a dime. In those days, new Columbia records cost thirty-five cents for the Red Label, fifty-five cents for the Green. Other popular labels were Victor, its cheaper subsidiary Bluebird (Glen Miller's label), and Decca (Bing Crosby's label). Columbia featured Harry James and later Frank Sinatra. New records were, then, very expensive for kids, and they broke easily, making the used record store very popular.

Granville South, from Broadway up to W15th Ave, was also a favourite shopping area though second to downtown. For the ladies, the pièce de résistance was Madame Runge's, which is gone now. There were other ladies' stores that I frankly don't remember.

I do remember the restaurants well. On the southwest corner of Broadway and Granville was the Aristocratic, commonly called the "Crat", there until the Indigo Chapters bookstore took over a few years ago. (There was another "Crat" at 41st and Granville, the haunt of the guys from nearby Vancouver College and girls who just happened to be passing by). Further up the street on the west side was the Normandy Cafe and at the corner of 15th, was the Blue Boy, where the PW kids hung out. Owned by a Mrs. Littler, it was impolitely called Littler's Lousy Lunch. How poor Mrs. Littler ever made any money is beyond me since she was lucky to get a nickel apiece for a Coca-Cola or two and, perhaps, as much as a dime in the jukebox, per customer, for her trouble. Both the Normandy and the Blue Boy are gone. At 16th was a Home Oil gas station run by one of Vancouver's characters, Hughie O'Callaghan, whose wife, Rene, was a champion golfer.

Across the street from the Normandy was, and remains, the Stanley Theatre. Every Thursday night it had a "preview", a movie showing for the first time in Vancouver and a secret until the projector rolled. This was very popular and the PW kids would move from the Blue Boy to the Normandy for the occasion. This brought them into contact with the King Edward High School kids for whom the Normandy was their hangout. PW and King Ed were bitter football rivals and, I'm sorry to say, these Thursday collisions sometimes resulted in fisticuffs ostensibly over football but, one suspects, more over girls.

On the east side of Granville, just south of the Stanley, was Thompson and Page, which sold records—in those days all 78s, either 10" or 12" and made of rather brittle wax. Shortly after the war the first "unbreakable" records came out and I recall buying one of the first, taking it up to the Hatfields' place where all the kids were gathered, and, showing off, threw it on the floor. It broke into God knows how many pieces! Thompson and Page replaced it.

At this time a great conundrum faced teenagers. The long play record came into vogue and Columbia had theirs going at 33 1/3 rpm, while Victor were at 45 rpm. This meant you had to select one of two styles of record players. I selected the Victor and it turned out to be the winner for the single song records. Columbia wound up with the much larger records and became the king of the album and all the classical music as a result.

During my last year of high school I wrote a column for the

Three Feathers school paper called "Rattling Records With Rafe". This led to my one and only brush with "graft" as the charming ladies at Thompson and Page would occasionally give me a record in order to get the publicity in my column! I'm glad to say no one uncovered this criminal activity in my later political days!

SPEAKING OF MUSIC ...

The English hate music but they love the noise it makes.
– Sir Thomas Beecham

When I was about ten, I started to get interested in music, popular variety.

First, it was the great Lancashire performer, George Formby, who played an instrument called the "banjuke" being, evidently, a combination of a banjo and a ukulele. He did very funny stuff like "Washing Windows" where he related some of the more pleasant scenes to greet the window washer doing his rounds. He did some movies, all comedies, of course, (I remember *It's In The Air*) which were "light" propaganda for the "war effort". He had a huge mouth and a face that constantly laughed. I loved him.

Gracie Fields, another Lancastrian, was extremely popular as she sang for the war effort so that listening to her was not only fun but considered a patriotic duty. Her great hit was any one of a number of "war songs" but I loved her humorous "The Biggest Aspidistra in the World". She did a very popular concert in Vancouver during the war. She became unpopular after she moved to the USA during the war even though Churchill had asked her to do so in order to raise US dollars for the war effort.

And there was the "Sweetheart of the Armed Forces", Vera Lynn, ninety-eight at this writing, about whom much more later.

My mother tried in vain to get me interested in classical music but, with the exception of Strauss waltzes, had little effect until I was much older. When I did discover classical I was astonished at how much Mom had taught me if only through osmosis.

By the time I was twelve, the swing bands of Glenn Miller, Tommy Dorsey, and Harry James dominated my listening and by war's end, this taste had morphed into Boogie Woogie with pianists like Albert Ammons, Pete Johnson, and Jack Fina, with the later addition of Freddy Slack. Pete Johnson did a couple of remarkable Boogie Woogie pieces called "Boo Woo" and "Woo Woo" with Harry James who played boogie with the trumpet. (His ability to play that and "The Flight of the Bumblebee" were proofs, in my mind, that he was the best trumpeter in the world. (This was before Winton Marsalis.) Vocalists Bing Crosby, Frank Sinatra, and Vaughan Monroe were big, and on the distaff side, Jo Stafford, Doris Day, and, always the greatest, Ella Fitzgerald.

Allow me to digress; the Palomar Supper Club, ran by Sandy de Santis, who also had the band, was where the Burrard Building now stands at 1030 W Georgia, and it held a Saturday matinee for kids at a dollar per show. One very hot summer day, Ella Fitzgerald was the star and there was probably a dozen of us who showed up. We naturally expected we would be given our dollar back and sent home; however, that was not to be. At the appointed moment the band struck up and Ella came out. She beckoned all of us to come up and sit on or near the stage and then, for two hours, with one short break, she sang almost every song we asked for. I, however, requested her big hit "My Happiness", which she refused to sing "because it was a ballad." I later found out that as big it was, she hated it because it was forced upon her by her agent who told her that she had to make some money instead of just doing what she wanted to. Similarly with the beautiful "Tea Leaves". What a day!

In a strange incident, I saw Ella again in the '70s at The Cave Supper Club and she had been quoted as saying that she had never been to Vancouver before. I reminded her of the Palomar but she stoutly denied it!

In recent years I've become enchanted with a couple of unknowns—Eva Cassidy and Thelma Gracen; both did great unnoticed stuff, the former being discovered shortly before her untimely death with Thelma just simply being unknown. I think I should include Gale Garnet who had but one hit, "We'll Sing in the Sunshine", a big hit of the '60s. Thanks to a friend I have a CD but I believe that's all she recorded, which is strange given her great singing.

At the end of the war, Les Brown and his Band of Renown and singer Doris Day hit the charts, big time, with "Sentimental Journey". Woody Herman and his various "Herds" were very popular too as was Stan Kenton and his singer, June Christy.

With the death of Glenn Miller in a plane crash in 1944, the big band era started its decline. It wasn't just Miller's death of course—bands were expensive, people listened more and more to radio and records, and TV started to eat into the bottom line.

Smaller groups came on the scene, notably the great Nat "King" Cole Trio whose big hit of 1946 was a song called "Nature Boy", brought to him by a strange bearded creature, allegedly out of the Hollywood Hills, named George Alexander Aberle who called himself eden ahbez (like the poet e.e. cummings he didn't use the upper case.) Aberle was an interesting cat and here's how Wikipedia puts it:

> *"ahbez", (born George Alexander Aberle in Brooklyn, New York on April 15, 1908; died March 4, 1995) was an American songwriter and recording artist from the 1940s-1960s, whose lifestyle in California was influential on the hippie movement.*
>
> *ahbez composed the song "Nature Boy", which became a #1 hit for eight weeks in 1948 for Nat "King" Cole, and has since become a pop and jazz standard.*
>
> *Living a bucolic life from at least the 1940s, he traveled in sandals and wore shoulder-length hair and beard, and white robes. He camped out below the first "L" in the Hollywood sign on the hill above Los Angeles, studied Oriental mysticism, and claimed to live on three dollars a week, sleeping outdoors with his family, and eating vegetables, fruits, and nuts.*

Jazz aficionados already knew of Cole as a magnificent jazz

pianist—a perennial All Star who, in his early days, was featured on Norman Granz's famous Jazz "At The Philharmonic" tours. But Cole had a wonderful crooning voice and style and moved away from Jazz into commercial stuff with enormous success. That was sad in a way, for a superb jazzman was lost. The great Canadian pianist Oscar Peterson once sang on an album but, when told he was a very good singer and should do more, he ended it there, saying, "I don't want to turn out like Nat Cole." He repeated and expanded on that when I interviewed him in 1982. Cole was the first of many small groups that became so popular in the '60s and '70s.

This is, strictly speaking, not true because groups like the Ink Spots and the Mills Brothers had been around since the '30s. Cole really inspired the sudden fashionableness of small groups like the Kingston Trio, the Lamplighters, the Crewcuts, the Page Cavanaugh Trio, and on they went.

Nat "King" Cole was truly a giant of his time, dying prematurely in 1965 just before his forty-fifth birthday. His daughter, Natalie, whose mother Marie Ellington sang with Duke Ellington (no relation), is a brilliant singer of the modern day and, wherever he is, Nat must be proud.

By the mid '40s I became what was to be a lifelong fan of "standard" jazz, especially presented by impresario Norman Granz and his "Jazz At The Philharmonic". They appeared several times at the old and gone Denman Auditorium as did, on a most memorable occasion, the triple-header of blind pianist George Shearing, Count Basie, and Billy Eckstine. The immediate postwar hero, Stan Kenton, appeared there as well with his very fine singer, June

Christy.

I was an early devotee of Bebop with Charlie Parker, Miles Davis, and Dizzy Gillespie (whom I had the honour of interviewing in 1982) but when it went down the Thelonius Monk route I didn't do the same. When I interviewed Dizzy it was a dialogue of the deaf as neither of us understood what the hell the other was talking about!

Ella Fitzgerald was my favourite female vocalist with Frankie Laine (before he got into that Wild Goose crap) my male favourite. There is a CD with Buck Clayton and Frankie Laine as the jazz vocalist, one of mine and Wendy's favourites of our 2,500 CDs. Have a listen—you'll be very pleasantly surprised, as was Dal Richards who only remembered Laine for the crap. Dal, in his late nineties, with his orchestra, continues to play more than 200 gigs a year.

There was a time I fancied myself a musical talent. The story is best told by fast forwarding to 1982 when I was doing a show on CJOR with a segment called "Mair's Memories". The idea was to have a "mystery" guest and see if listeners could recognize him or her.

One day my guest was Arthur Delamont, who founded and led the famous Kitsilano Boys Band, which did worldwide concerts. Mr. Delamont was in his nineties but sharp as a knife. When he was "found out" I said, "Mr. Delamont, I was one of your early failures ..."

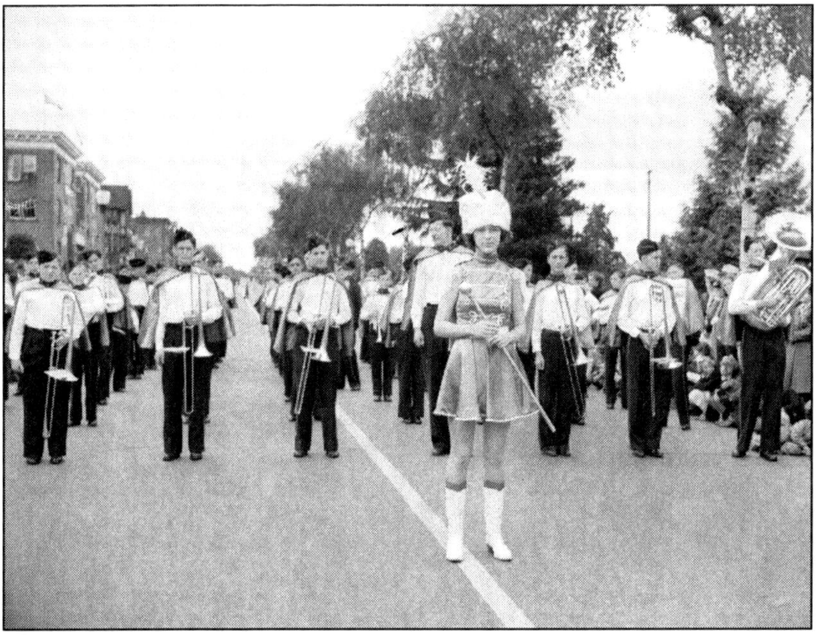

Kitsilano Boys Band 1939.

Our resident billionaire, Jimmy Pattison played trumpet.

Photo courtesy of the City of Vancouver Archives

"Now I know you! You're Ken Mair's boy who came to see me with a cornet in hand wanting to be Harry James the next day. I sent you home and never saw you again!"

That had indeed happened. My mom had gone downtown to a pawnbroker and got a cornet for $10 (a fair sum then). I was astonished that I couldn't get it to even make a sound and I wanted to quit, just like with the piano a little time before when I quit after one lesson because I couldn't play immediately with two hands! Mom persisted and I was despatched to Mr. Delamont's place. After one session, he assured my mother that I had no patience, nor any talent, hidden or otherwise.

I think Mom managed to get her $10 back!

If I had to pick one album to take with me to that desert island it would be Benny Goodman and his quartet with himself on clarinet, Teddy Wilson on piano, Gene Krupa on drums, and the incomparable Lionel Hampton on vibes.

I'm fortunate to have seen many of my musical heroes and interviewed a few; Lionel Hampton, King Cole, Frankie Laine (three times), the Mills Brothers (countless times), The Ink Spots, Ella Fitzgerald (twice), Louis Armstrong, Jack Teagarden, Buddy Rich, Count Basie, Dizzy Gillespie, Oscar Peterson, George Shearing, Billy Eckstine, Sarah Vaughn, Lena Horne, Louis Jordan, Mel Torme, Benny Goodman, and Billy Daniels (with whom I played a game of golf).

I didn't abandon popular music entirely in the '60s and still enjoy The Poppy Family—Terry and Susan Jacks, both British Columbians—The Everly Brothers, Simon and Garfunkle, the Manhattan Transfer, The Mommas and the Poppas, and especially ABBA. (Wendy and I have seen the stage performance of *Mamma Mia* in London eight times! Wendy continues to watch the movie whenever she can.)

In my dotage I've discovered classical music though I'm a long way from knowing much about it. I have one eight-gig iPod devoted to it. I have two two-gig iPods, two four-gigs, and an eight-gig. This is a huge advance in electronics—with all those CDs it would be well nigh impossible to play what you want to hear.

Today, as the CD quickly fades from view in favour of downloading from a computer, I haunt the CD websites and shops, especially in London, looking for the bargains from my childhood and youth of which there are many and which then go straight to the appropriate iPod.

My foray into classical music has me listening to Classic FM radio out of London. This is tricky because their rules confine them to the UK and won't let you listen if you don't live there. The trick is to use a UK postal code—I use our favourite hotel's. After a time I'll get a notice saying that I apparently don't live in the UK with a space to enter my proper postal code. I just re-do The Kensington Hotel and I'm back in business. Through this station I learned of a terrific British composer, Jon Lord, who was a huge rock and roll star with the group Deep Purple. You'll love his classical stuff! At this moment I'm listening to "Composer" by Sir Anthony Hopkins, the movie star, and to my ears he is very good indeed. Classic FM is a neat background for when I'm writing.

There are many other classical stations—KING in Seattle and KBGH out of Boston, for example, but they do too much interviewing and fund drives to suit my requirements. I suppose, preferring Classic FM, I'm a lawbreaker and one day will be arrested at Heathrow for my ongoing crime of "outside listening" and lying about my postal code.

I'll take my chances!

WHERE DID WE DO OUR MUSIC THING?

Dancing: the vertical expression of a horizontal desire legalized by music.

– George Bernard Shaw

Kids: they dance before they learn there is anything that isn't music.

– William Stafford

We had, at Prince of Wales, the usual assortment of school dances, probably about five or six per year. One of them, particularly popular with the girls, was the Sadie Hawkins dance, which came from the comic strip *Li'l Abner* and the story of how Sadie Hawkins' father, annoyed that his rather plain daughter could never get a date, created a day where girls could ask boys out instead of the customary other way around.

The big dance was, of course, the grad dance. Ours was done

by way of a draw and it was cruelty personified as boys would take insurance against drawing certain girls. It was an awful way to do it. It was supposed to ensure that every girl had a date. Even then I wasn't sure what made us boys think that we were all a delight to behold to the ladies who might be stuck with us. They were sufficiently lady-like not to have an insurance scheme of their own. After the dance had finished, boyfriends and girlfriends managed to meet at a post-grad party, which traditionally went on until dawn. I rather suspect that many hitherto intact virginities of both sexes were taken care of at that point.

There were also "mixers" at noon, and I can recall the principal, Mr. MacKenzie, calling me into his office and informing me that mixers were not intended to be "necking" contests. I'm sure Mr. MacKenzie was right in terms of the intention; however, these were scarcely mixers in any dictionary sense. They were opportunities for boyfriends and girlfriends to get together and neck, or for boys to prowl and look for girls to neck with. I suppose one could equate prowling to mixing.

A favourite was at St John's Anglican Church, at 27th and Granville, which had what was known as the "Saturday Night Club" in the parish hall. It was extremely popular and run by the Reverend Norman Larmonth. It was the "in" place to go on a Saturday night. Rules against liquor were strict yet somehow never successfully enforced. In fact, in a perverse way it always seemed that the harder the authorities tried to keep liquor away from teenage parties, the more there was.

I had an interesting personal experience along that line. I had brought six bottles of beer and half a bottle of rye whiskey in the trunk of my car. As I went out to have a beer with a pal, I was suddenly confronted by two of Vancouver's finest and, after opening my trunk, they charged me with being a juvenile in possession of liquor.

In due course I appeared in court, with my father, and was fined $10. What was interesting was that the beer was offered in evidence but the rye whiskey was nowhere to be seen. I wonder where it went?

Other churches of different faiths had similar institutions.

One could also go places like the Palladium in White Rock, or the Alma Academy at Broadway and Alma for "foreign" excitement. There was a gang, the Alma Dukes, at the Alma Academy and one ran the risk of getting into a fight. I was consistently a dedicated coward so I avoided the Alma Academy in favour of safer sites.

There were, of course, always house parties, which were popular or not depending upon how well they were chaperoned. Those held at the Hatfields' home were very popular indeed.

I CHANGE SCHOOLS

True terror is to wake up one morning and discover that your high school class is running the country.
– Kurt Vonnegut

By the time puberty struck, I was hankering to go to a school that had girls. I particularly wanted to go to Prince of Wales because at the "Island" I met and became friends with so many PW kids that I felt a part of them. The problem was I lived in another district (Magee) and needed a special dispensation to go to PW.

I visited the Superintendent of Schools, Mr. McCorkindale, who allowed me to cross the line. Mr. McCorkindale had a lovely daughter, Mary, who married one of my good friends, Gordon Christopher, at one point the president of our fraternity.

I was very pleased to leave St George's although I did derive some good from it, of course, especially good study habits enforced with the constant fear of that damned cane!

When I got to PW it was like heaven. A lot of the kids I had known as far back as Maple Grove, indeed Jack and Jill Kindergarten, to say nothing of Bill Stuart, Meryl Fraser, the Milroys, Doug Fripps—the "Island" gang—who were there and I had no trouble fitting in immediately. David Owen took me under his wing and in no time I was playing soccer and going to the school mixers. In fact, in my first month at PW in Grade X, I was elected to the School Council. I served as school Treasurer in Grade XII, spawning a bit of a story ...

The teacher to whom I was responsible was Russ Robinson, a pretty neat guy but very punctilious about money down to the penny. As a matter of fact, he was as close to a nickel as skin is to bone. In chemistry class, we found that if you put a penny into sulphuric acid, you could reduce it to the size of a dime. This meant that you could put the "dime" into the Coca-Cola machine (for which as Treasurer I was responsible) and receive a Coca-Cola and three pennies, which, of course, could then be converted into three more ersatz dimes. When Mr. Robinson discovered this scam, he was horrified, although my protestations of innocence, while I'm sure not believed, carried the day.

I remember on my first day at my new school I went downtown and bought myself a PW sweater, then repaired to the Blue Boy Café on South Granville where all of the PW kids congregated. I couldn't wait to become one of them. PW was a very small school and had tremendous school spirit. We obviously couldn't compete in sports on an equal basis with the larger schools but we played against them and, from time to time, beat them, which was a time of enormous rejoicing.

One of my classmates was John Fraser, later the Speaker of the House of Commons. John was generally a pretty quiet, sober kid but I remember him in English class when he loosened the hinges of the huge oak door of the cloakroom and English teacher, Lacey Fisher, came in one morning with his customary hangover, opened the door, and was, of course, flattened. John and I were Environment Ministers at the same time, he federally and I provincially, and have remained lifelong friends—and environmentalists.

I have always felt very grateful that I had the chance to go to PW, now sadly moved to where the eighth hole used to be at the old Quilchena Golf Club and now a pretty big high school. The old school, in the words of a pal, Al Taylor, was like a co-educational private school. The new school's most illustrious grad is former Prime Minister Kim Campbell.

MOVIES, COMICS, AND STUFF

I don't remember when exactly I read my first comic book, but I do remember exactly how liberated and subversive I felt as a result.
– Edward W. Said

When I was a pre-teen, my theatre was the Kerrisdale on 41st Avenue near The Boulevard, where we all went for the Saturday afternoon movie. It cost a dime; when a wartime luxury tax came in it went to twelve cents, requiring a plea for an increase in allowance!

Often the theatre would put on a contest for the kids—a yo-yo or maybe a bolo bat contest. They were very popular but I was lousy at both. There was invariably a serial, an adventure story, which, like soaps on radio, moved so slowly that if you missed a few episodes you could pick up the thread easily. The one that comes instantly to mind was *King of the Royal Mounted*. There was always a cartoon, perhaps a Disney or maybe Bugs Bunny, and a newscast, plus a trailer for a coming movie. I remember a lot of the movies but, mercifully, I've forgotten a hell of a lot more.

It was the beginning of Walt Disney starting with *Mickey Mouse* but moving into extravaganzas like *Snow White and the Seven Dwarfs*—at kids' parties I always seemed to play Grumpy, which was marginally better than Dopey—then came *Bambi, Pinocchio, Dumbo,* and the classical-music-based *Fantasia*. Disney cartoons arrived, featuring Mickey, girlfriend Minnie, Goofy, Horace Horsecollar, Clarabell the Cow, Donald Duck and his squeeze Daisy, and Uncle McScrooge and nephews Hughie, Dewey, and Louie.

I remember smarmy little Shirley Temple and her nauseating songs like "Playmate", "Little Sir Echo", and "On The Good Ship Lollypop". I especially remember being taken, against my will, to the film version of Heidi. I hated it. Shirley Temple was for dames, not red-blooded little boys.

There were the animal stories (*Black Beauty, My Friend Flicka,* and *Lassie Come Home* to name a few) and scads of war movies starring valiant Americans like John Wayne who bravely slaughtered the Japanese and took the Pacific Islands singlehandedly. In reality, Wayne spent the entire war dodging the draft while Jimmy Stewart, Clark Gable, and Douglas Fairbanks, Jr. fought with distinction. The best war picture was British, *In Which We Serve,* starring Noel Coward and a young Richard Attenborough who played a young seaman who lost his nerve in battle. Fifty years later I interviewed the now Lord Attenborough and greeted him, "I remember you as a snivelling little coward!" He laughed, obviously not offended, and insisted, "Call me Dick." Close behind was *Mrs. Miniver* with Walter Pidgeon and Greer Garson.

The most memorable adult movies for me were *How Green Was My Valley, Gone With The Wind,* and just as I reached that "certain age", *National Velvet,* starring every twelve-year-old's heartthrob, Elizabeth Taylor. Actually, I fell in love with quite a few stars—Betty Grable, Rita Hayworth, the swimmer Esther Williams, Hedy Lamarr, and especially, Joan Leslie (now forgotten, it seems).

Just in time for puberty, Howard Hughes gave us *The Outlaw* where, in a shocking scene that sent preachers into a swoon, Jane Russell bent over a mirror and exposed her boobs almost down to the nipples. The movie's promo was "How would you like to tussle with Russell?"

Comic strips (books) were big. The spread of World War II to America had a profound cultural impact on us kids. Suddenly American comics took on a new meaning as comic books like *True Comics* and *Real Heroes,* which concentrated on the War, American version, became popular. You only had to read *True Comics* or *Real Heroes* to learn history, US style, for these comics gave an American sanitized view of the great issues of the time, meaning we got their bullshit and not that of Britain.

Little Orphan Annie, that insipid waif with the blank eyes, and a tiresome mongrel named Sandy who said "arf" every other frame, was for all that, hugely popular. Her "step-father", Daddy Warbucks, was stinking rich with a sparkling diamond as a shirt stud and a cheap bastard who was nowhere to be found when Annie most needed a bit of money. Rounding out the group were the Asp, a shadowy figure who always looked like he'd just stepped out of a high class cat-house, and Punjab, a large turbaned Indian with a huge sword on his belt. Evidently he was a mute. Annie did her bit for the war effort by forming the Junior G-Men (not Junior G-Persons, you will note) and God knows how we would have won the war without her, as she, with Sandy, rounded up all the German spies in the country. She also, for a box top from some breakfast cereal and a dime (to cover shipping and handling, we were told), would send you a simulated airplane control panel so that you could learn to fly at home and be ready for combat duty. Her favourite exclamation was "leapin' lizards". The comic morphed into the highly successful musical *Annie*.

There was the highly improbable *Superman* (stolen from Canadian artist, Joe Schuster) who was bullet proof, could fly, indeed do anything: one wondered why he wasn't in the war, ending it in a trice. Superman came from a distant planet, Krypton, and masqueraded as mild-mannered Clark Kent who, with his apparently virginal squeeze Lois Lane, were reporters for the *Daily Planet*. When the call for action arose, Clark would hop into the nearest phone booth (remember them?) and remove his street clothes becoming Superman in a blue suit with a big yellow "S" on it. Where his clothes went was never explained. Eventually it was decided that Superman's absence from the war had to be explained. It seems that when Clark Kent took his physical, by mistake he had his X-Ray vision on and read the eye chart in the next room in a most understandable error (?), so he failed.

Somehow we swallowed that gup!

We read *Captain Marvel*, really Billy Batson, a corner newsboy (remember them?) in drag. He was a Superman knock-off. There were *Batman and Robin* and the evil *The Penguin*, who made a huge mark when TV arrived. There was *Mandrake the Magician* with his companion, Lothar, who was a former African chief and, like Superman, impervious to harm although he couldn't fly.

More in the peaceful mode were *The Katzenjammer Kids* who lived in some remote African jungle with the Captain and his wife—a favourite strip, which, over an artist's dispute, split in two with the other one called *The Captain and the Kids*. There was *Li'l Abner*, the empty-headed hillbilly hulk sired by a toothless old fart, Pappy Yokum, and borne by an old bat named Mammy Yokum. Abner's innocent but bountifully built fair maiden was Daisy Mae and eventually they were hitched by Marryin' Sam who, as his pièce de résistance, did his $2 wedding. Other residents of the Yokum hometown of Dogpatch were Earthquake McGoon, Moonbeam McSwine, and B.O. Plenty. The latter married Gravel Gertie, who presented him with a nauseating little girl called "Sparkle" Plenty. The artist was the brilliant satirist, Al Capp, who from time to time would lampoon Chester Gould's *Dick Tracy* in a spoof called *Fearless Fosdick* (the artist was scarcely anonymous, being called Lester Gooch). Fosdick, despite being shot full of holes most of the time, managed to make himself useful in fighting crime. Li'l Abner became a very funny and popular musical. Capp got himself into trouble when he lampooned

Pepsi-Cola using the slogan "Pepsi-Cola hits the spot, puts you six feet under and that's a lot!" and "The pause that petrifies". Capp was sued successfully for a substantial amount of money. Interestingly, the courts have banned publication of the facts to this day, evidently on the petition of Pepsi, so you'll have to rely upon my memory.

Dick Tracy, modern before his time, had a two-way radio wristwatch so could receive instructions and give orders. Some of the baddies he dealt with were FruitFly, Prune Face, Flattop Jones, and Larceny Lu. He never got around to marrying his ever-faithful Tess.

There was the popular *Moon Mullins*, with Kayo, his urchin kid brother, and their landlord and landlady, Lord and Lady Plushbottom. Then there was Joe Palooka, the boxer who was the "Great White Hope" when that was an acceptable term, and his manager, Knobby Walsh. A bit of trivia: in the movie *Joe Palooka*, Joe was played by Joe Kirkwood Jr., whose Dad was Joe Kirkwood Sr., the famous trick shot golfer, whom my Dad took me to see when I was a kid. Joe Jr. was a professional on the PGA Tour.

Smitty was the story of an office boy named ... Smitty. Every year his boss went up to the "North Woods" to fish, and every year hooked "old fighter", a huge salmon, and every year found a way to lose him.

Big Chief Wahoo was an Indian (according to Buffy Sainte-Marie, "Indian" is what Native Americans usually call themselves) who struck oil and spent his time flitting around with a W.C. Fields- type character and his, Wahoo's, niece Minnie Ha-Cha.

He eventually hooked up with a New York reporter, Steve Roper. Gradually Big Chief Wahoo was written out of the strip and Steve Roper took over.

The best one for, mostly, boys was surely *Terry and the Pirates*, by Milt Caniff. Terry battled for good over evil in what was then French Indo-China, now Vietnam. There was the evil Dragon Lady (who as the war advanced, changed sides) and other strange people such as Big Stoop, Captain Judas, Cherry Blaze, Chopstick Joe, Cue Ball, and Dude Hennick. After the war, Caniff left *Terry and the Pirates* and started *Steve Canyon*, and another gung ho American flyboy was born.

Air travel was all the rage and fliers (US variety, of course) were our big heroes. Planes captured the imagination with two very popular strips; *Tailspin Tommy*, who flew dangerous missions to makeshift air strips in the Andes, and *Smilin' Jack*, with his pal Downwind (who was always shown half face), who also faced fearful odds in bringing help and justice to those who needed it. Air travel moved into space with *Buck Rogers* in the 25th Century AD and *Flash Gordon*. Not to be forgotten is *Tom Swift And His Airship*.

Looking at the other side of time was *Alley Oop*, a caveman who found himself in the jungles of Moo and surrounded by hungry dinosaurs. Dinny, the dinosaur who quickly became his pet, was the principal means of transportation for Oop while in Moo.

In the "goofy" genre none was goofier than *Smokey Stover*, the fireman.

The puns and "silly pictures on the wall with various items hanging clear out of the frames" was the feature that provoked the most interest, which the author Bill Holman called "wallnuts". (Example: A picture of a fish opening a door is labeled "Calling cod"; my favourite showed two sailors at the door asking the mother if "Anchor was home," to which she replied, "Anchor's away, my boys.")

Also on the amusing side, the perpetual *Blondie* and Dagwood with Alexander, then known as "Baby Dumpling", were there, as were Maggie and Jiggs with "daughter", in *Bringing Up Father*. Jiggs was an Irish-American who had gone from rags to riches but still liked to meet the boys on the cranes for lunch of corned beef and ... (cabbage was never spelt out for some reason).

Our Boarding House with Major Hoople, the loveable phoney, featured his fierce wife Martha, Nephew Alvin, and boarders three, Twigg, Clyde, and Mac. This was my favourite.

Tim Tyler, another of my favourites, was drawn by Lyman Young, brother of Chic Young who did *Blondie*. Tim started out in an orphanage but I best remember him and his pal Spud and their high adventures in wildest Africa.

There was *Popeye* with Olive Oyl, Mr. Geezil, and the bum, Wimpy, who was the hamburger eater's equivalent of an alcoholic; there was *Tillie the Toiler*, the secretary who joined the army in World War II amongst other adventures and was loved in vain by Mac, the runty office boy; and the beginnings of *Pogo*, the best satirical comic of all time, in my view, created by Walt Kelly. In the fifties, I began my lifetime dislike of the *Vancouver Sun*, which, because *Pogo* had criticized the newly minted hero Fidel Castro, pulled the comic. The comic strip equivalent of the soppy soap suds heroine was *Mary Worth*, a tiresome old do-gooder who travelled about spouting wisdom with a sickening benign smile for all, good or bad.

Perhaps the most enduring was *Gasoline Alley* featuring Walt and Phyllis Wallet who, finding a baby on their doorstep, adopted him and named him Skeezix (don't ask me!). This comic stayed in the present so everyone aged and ultimately died. Brother Corky grew up in the saga as did sister Judy. Nina Clock (brought up by grandparents *Grandfather* Clock—naturally—and wife) was Skeezix's sweetie. Wilmer Bobble, the tainted alderman, was once Skeezix's business partner. About the time the war ended, Skeezix, who had served in the Pacific (Wilmer dodged the draft) married Nina. When the characters began to die off, so did the strip.

There were many cowboy strips and I think of *Ken Maynard*, the first I recall, *Gene Autry, Hopalong Cassidy, Roy Rogers, Tom Mix, The Lone Ranger and Tonto*, and *Red Ryder* with Little Beaver, his sidekick. Many were more famous on the screen and radio than for their comic strips.

I have only scratched the surface but these are the ones I remember reading as a kid. Comics were more than just fun to read. We learned a lot from them, most of it ranging from questionable in value to harmful.

Racial prejudices were planted early, making them difficult to later cast aside. In the racial comic strips, Japanese were "Japs", Germans were "Krauts", and Chinese "Chinks". Wrongs were made into right: such as the Filipinos, it was said, just loved the American occupation going back to the Spanish-American War, which freed them from the Spaniards; just as the Vietnamese loved their French masters and African Blacks adored the British. That these occupations were detested was carefully overlooked.

Comic strips provided a plethora of things kids could join, as the heroes had organizations galore. You were counselled to join with *Red Ryder* and get a BB gun from the Daisy company; learn to fly by mail and help beat the Axis; and for ten cents and a box top (or facsimile of same) you could be a representative of clean living and become a buddy of *Jack Armstrong, the All-American Boy.*

I mustn't leave it here since there were three book series that were really like comics, and starting with the highly influential works of fiction for kids: *The Hardy Boys, Frank and Joe,* for boys, and *Nancy Drew,* for girls. Both specialized in high, improbable adventure, as did *Don Winslow,* a US Naval Commander who, with his sidekick Red Pendleton, won the Second World War amongst other adventures. One time they corralled a German spy named Pfeffer who had stolen a US Navy blueprint for diverting the Gulf Stream. Now the Nazis could freeze Britain to death. Never mind how this little handheld gadget could handle this task; unanswered also was what would happen to Pfeffer's Nazi Germany without the Gulf Stream? Ah, well, you had to be able to overlook little details like that!

Then there were the radio shows, many of which also were comic strips that I mention above. *Superman* comes to mind in that regard; "Look! Look! Up in the sky! It's a bird! It's a plane! It's Superman?" So does *Terry and The Pirates*. A favourite was *Jack Armstrong, the All-American Boy,* brought to you by Wheaties, the

Breakfast of Champions.

One of my favourite radio shows was *Gangbusters,* a youngsters' show sponsored interestingly enough by Philip Morris Cigarettes. Another was the *Green Hornet,* with Kato, his loyal Filipino servant, and his wildly modern vehicle, Black Beauty, all brilliantly lampooned by Peter Sellers in the *Pink Panther* series.

There were spooky shows like *The Shadow, Inner Sanctum, Suspense,* and *The Whistler.* I especially remember one dark night at the Island. There was a summer thunderstorm and a bunch of us early teens listened to *Inner Sanctum.* We were sure we could hear movement on the roof and someone trying to get in a window. It was "theatre of the mind" at its best.

We listened to radio as a family on Sunday evenings to our favourites including Jack Benny, Fred Allen, Edgar Bergen, and Charlie McCarthy. Very popular was *Take it or Leave It* where servicemen (mostly) could actually make $64! After the $32 mark was passed the moderator, Phil Baker, would ask if the contestant wanted to try for $64. If he answered "yes" there was always a voice that rang out "You'll be sorry!" Somehow whenever a contestant said he was from Brooklyn it brought big applause. This morphed into the TV show *The $64,000 Question,* which flamed out in scandal in 1958. Incidentally, two of Phil Baker's children live in Greater Vancouver and the son, Michael Conway Baker, is a well-known composer. Another very popular show was *Amos and Andy,* a highly stereotyped take-off on Blacks in Harlem. I've often wondered how funny we would think this show today.

There were other shows, of course. There was *Abbott and*

Costello, Bud and Lou, whose wit was rather corny but they were very popular. I remember two things very well. They did a bit on baseball called "Who's On First", which remains a classic. (It's lots of fun and easy to Google.) The other episode came when Bud Abbot, after a show, told us that Lou Costello's child had drowned in a swimming pool that morning but that Lou said, "The show must go on."

There were midweek shows like *Jack Carson,* what we would now call a sit-com, *Burns and Allen* comedians, and *Ozzie and Harriet.* A very popular show was "Lux Radio Theatre" featuring the famous Hollywood director Cecil B. DeMille, which started out with "Lux presents Hollywood!"

There were more highbrow shows like *Information Please* and the *Whiz Kids.* I hated those little brats who knew so much, especially Joel Kuperman who lisped but always lisped the right answer.

Things we joined ... In the '40s and '50s there was a sort of Freemasonry for kids. For example, the *Vancouver Sun* had a club for kids called Uncle Ben's while the *Province* had the Tillicums. I was a Tillicum because you got a neat genuine fake silver totem pole pin. The password was "Kla-howya" which, according to cousin Hugh, was pigeon English for a native saying as he entered the Hudson's Bay Store, "Clerk, how are you." That sounded like a bit of a stretch to me but I have never heard a better explanation. The third Vancouver paper, the morning *News Herald,* had no club. Whichever club you belonged to, you sneered at members of the other as lesser breeds. I remember Shelly's 4X Bread had a club but have forgotten the details.

Then there was Charles Atlas telling how he was once a ninety-eight-pound weakling picked on by bullies who, at the beach, in front of his girlfriend, kicked sand in his face. This need never happen to you if you followed his instructions how to build a great body through "Dynamic Tension". You could join for a dime. Lots of us did but Locarno Beach did not suddenly become noted for great physiques on young teenage boys.

The offer I never took up for fear my mom found out was a neat little gizmo called a Vacutex, with which you could suck out blackheads of which I had a plethora.

There was no shortage of things to join and we did, mostly for ten cents, and our commitment lasted about as long the dime did.

ENTER THE IDIOTIC BOX

I find television very educating. Every time somebody turns on the set, I go into the other room and read a book.
– Groucho Marx

Let's have a look at television—if we really must.

We weren't the first to have a TV in Vancouver but not far behind it; we first got one in 1951 and in a curious way. An appliances company on the Boulevard in Kerrisdale (a Vancouver suburb), Fred Walsh and Sons, had the rights to a brand of TV. TV was very much in its infancy and they needed to show it off in their premises to prospective buyers. In those days you needed a very tall aerial even if you lived on top of a hill, which we did at 5629 Angus Drive. Walsh and Sons asked to run a wire from their store, a couple of miles away, and put an aerial on our roof in exchange for which they would put a TV set in our den and leave it there for the duration of their promotion.

Dad was away at the time but Mom reluctantly agreed. When Dad came home and saw the aerial he was furious—until, like us, he viewed the TV and got hooked.

There was no cable across the US, let alone Canada, then and all we could pick up was Channel 5 out of Seattle. In short order, however, we could get KOMO Seattle, then KCTS from Tacoma, and finally KVOS from Bellingham. All the US national networks of the day were soon covered.

In 1952, the coaxial cable came to the US west coast, which meant live shows from the eastern US. The first major live events we saw were the 1952 Democratic and Republican conventions that saw Adlai Stevenson and Dwight Eisenhower selected as presidential candidates. Suddenly, as if by magic, we could watch live sporting events like baseball and NFL football, the Kentucky Derby, and even the occasional hockey game. The man who became my big hero, Edward R. Murrow, was there on CBS at 6:00 p.m. on weeknights.

There was first class entertainment on various playhouses like *Playhouse 90* and excellent vaudeville shows—the world stopped at 5:00 p.m. on Sunday evening to watch the *Ed Sullivan Show* or Steve Allen who, in my opinion, was far better. There was good comedy like Sid Caesar and Imogene Coca, George Gobel, and later, the *Smothers Brothers* and the *Rowan & Martin's Laugh-In* with Flip Wilson playing the black lady, Geraldine, whose by-line was, "What you sees is what you gets." One of the funniest was Carol Burnett with Tim Conway and Harvey Korman, the latter two in *The Dentist*, which remains a great and very funny classic.

Somebody got a bright idea. Why didn't apartment buildings have one aerial that serviced all the suites for a small amount each month! It was called TruView, the precursor to Cablevision. At that point, TV was as good as it would ever be. With four channels we had ABC, NBC, and CBS, all live. It was great and I watched it a lot. Even the sitcoms like *Mr. Peepers*, *Ozzie and Harriet* (with their son Ricky who was to become a big music star in his own right), and *Our Miss Brooks* with Eve Arden were good fun.

Then on 1 July 1958, the CBC made an immense fuss about extending their signal from coast to coast. For most in Vancouver, this meant very little if anything. To listen to the CBC, however, you would have thought that we were a TV wasteland until they mercifully arrived to our assistance. Ottawa played it up as gloriously enhancing national unity. It has been all downhill since then. TV has proved the Comedian Fred Allen to be right when he called it, "Chewing gum for the eyes."

In 1980, the federal government, true to its pledge to make us all love Canadian TV whether we wanted to or not, banned the use of satellite dishes that enabled people to watch many new American productions, especially films. My former colleague, Dr. Patrick McGeer remarked, fairly I thought, that if they didn't want him to watch satellite television, they should stop beaming it at his front lawn.

I decided to challenge the law and had a dish installed at our house, and then had a party for which I charged a $1 admission so that I was doing this professionally. I wrote out a confession and sent it to the minister, Francis Fox, and demanded to be charged.

I heard nothing and the whole issue died, as it should have, assuming that any government was stupid enough to get involved in it in the first place.

Appalling as TV now is, my greater complaint is the channel changer. *This* is what I want: the ability to change channels, adjust the sound, and turn the TV off and on. Anything more is an invention too far. The options I now have bewilder me and have nothing to do with what I want to watch.

Now, I am a world class klutz. I haven't the vaguest idea how a TV or, indeed, a computer works nor am I much interested in finding out. When I am going to watch TV, a very rare event, Wendy hollers, "Don't for God's sake turn it on, let me do it!" But I'm a proud man so I press the power button and everything then unravels. Weird things happen on the screen. I'm asked questions, shown menus, and given options. Wendy arrives but it's too late. I call Shaw Cable who patiently walks me through the steps necessary to watch. I believe they have a voice recognition system at Shaw, and when I phone they draw straws to see who gets me!

I watch little TV—baseball and a good English comedy is about all and that's plenty enough.

SLOGANS OF THE '40S

Love your enemies. It makes them so damned mad.

– P.D. East

When we were kids, billboards and slogans were all the rage. Today, a new billboard causes neighbourhoods to rise as one and city councils to be besieged with angry citizens, but they were so prevalent when I was young. Ogden Nash, the famous American humourist/poet, was prompted to write this parody of Joyce Kilmer's "Trees":

> "I think that I shall never see
> A billboard lovely as a tree
> Indeed unless the billboards fall
> I'll never see a tree at all."

Not all billboards were offensive. Burmashave shaving cream used to have small signs on the side of the road spaced about 100 yards apart, five in number. They were great fun to spot and read when I was a child traveling to Seattle. One example:

“Heed our school
Zone instructions
Protect our little
Tax deductions
BURMASHAVE”

Or,

“Ashes to ashes
Dust to dust
Keep Washington green
Or we’ll all go bust.
BURMASHAVE”

Slogans on billboards were often jingles on the radio. They could be fun but would be played over and over to the point where your teeth would grind.

Here are some slogans and jingles I can remember. Those of a certain age may find it fun to play a sort of trivia by trying to remember their own!

“From contented cows.” – Borden’s milk

"For a treat, not a treatment, Old Gold." – Lorillard cigarettes

"More doctors smoke Camels than any other cigarette." – Reynolds Tobacco

"Phone To Morrow for your coal today." – Morrow Ice and Coal

"So round, so full, so fully packed, so free and easy on the draw." – Lucky Strike cigarettes

"The soap of beautiful women." – Camay

"Bee Yo (B.O.)" – Lifebuoy Soap

"Ask the man who owns one." – Packard cars

"When better cars are built, Buick will build them." – GM

"See the USA, in your Chevrolet." – GM

"Oxydol's own Ma Perkins." – Proctor & Gamble

"The man of distinction." – Lord Calvert's (Seagrams)

"Don't spill a drop!" – Old Smuggler Whiskey

"We hae meat that ye can eat." – James Inglis Reid meats

"We could have priced it higher." – Canadian Club whiskey

"From zero to 30 in 10 seconds." – Nash Motors

"Freshen up with 7-Up." – Pepsi-Cola

"Things go better with Coke." – Coca Cola

"This Bud's for you." – Budweiser Beer

"Ford has a better idea." – Ford Motors

"They'll know you've arrived when you drive up in an Edsel." – Ford Motors (Man! Did that ever turn out to be true!)

"Valley of the Jolly Green Giant, Ho, Ho, Ho." – General Mills

"From Everest to the everyday." – Grape Nuts

"Our main objective is customer satisfaction." – Barbasol shaving cream

"Good to the very last drop." – Maxwell House Coffee

"It tastes awful, but it works." – Buckley's Cough Syrup

"Halo is the shampoo that glorifies your hair." – Halo Shampoo

"Winstons taste good like a cigarette should." - Reynolds Tobacco Co.

"How are you fixed for blades?" – Gillette Blue Blades

"If you've got the time, we've got the beer." – Miller High Life

"ABC, Always Buy Chesterfields." – Liggett & Myers

"I go for a man who wears an Adams Hat." – Adams Hats

"Old Spice means quality, said the Captain to the Bos'un." – Old Spice shaving lotion

"It's Lucky when you live in the West." – Lucky Lager beer

"Secure the shadow ere the substance fades." – Kerrisdale Cameras

"Tide's in, dirt's out." – Proctor & Gamble

"To keep presentable longer." – Mennen shaving cream, Colgate

"A little dab'll do ya." – Brylcreem, Unilever

"Look sharp! Feel sharp! Be sharp!" – Gillette razors

"For your pet, you'd better get ..." – Dr. Ballard's Dog Food

"The family that prays together, stays together." – Catholic Church

"D-U-Z spells DUZ ... DUZ does it!" – Duz Soap (the joke was F-U-G spells FUG ... If DUZ won't do it, FUG it!) – Proctor & Gamble

"You'd better get Wildroot Cream Oil Charlie." – Colgate-Palmolive jingle made popular by the King Cole Trio

"The pause that refreshes." – Coca-Cola

"Alas! My poor brother." – Bovril sign in Piccadilly Circus, London

"Don't be vague, say Haig and Haig!" – Haig and Haig Scotch

"What'll you have ..." – Pabst Blue Ribbon

"Goebel's is mellowized for you." – Goebels Beer

"The beer that made Milwaukee famous." – Schlitz Beer

"Buy Bonds and stamps to lick the tramps and send your old watch to Grassie's." – Grassie Jeweller's

"If Grassie's can't repair your watch, throw it away!" – Grassie Jeweller's

"The home of friendly jewellery." – Peoples Credit Jewellers

"99 and 44 100ths % pure." – Ivory Soap, Proctor & Gamble

"Rinso White! Rinso White! Happy Little Washday Song." – Unilever

"Floats the dirt right down the drain." – Ajax, the foaming cleanser, Colgate

"Quaker puffed wheat sparkies, the wheat that's shot from guns." – Quaker Oats

"The breakfast of champions." – Wheaties

"Snap, Crackle, Pop." – Kellogg's Rice Krispies

"Not for years, not for life but guaranteed forever." – Eversharp

"On your wrist as on the air, faithful forever." – Bulova Watch

"Lux presents Hollywood." – Lux soap

"You can have money as near as your phone." – Local Loan

"You'll wonder where the yellow went." – Pepsodent tooth paste

"$1.49 day Tuesday!" – Woodward's stores

TOUCH NOT ONE BLADE OF YON GREEN GRASS

A strange thing is memory, and hope; one looks backward, and the other forward; one is of today, the other of tomorrow. Memory is history recorded in our brain, memory is a painter, it paints pictures of the past and of the day. – Anna Mary Robertson Moses

I'd give all wealth that years have piled,
The slow result of Life's decay,
To be once more a little child
For one bright summer-day.
– Lewis Carroll

The jewel of Vancouver, then as now, was Stanley Park.

Stanley Park, a peninsula, juts out into inner and outer Vancouver harbour. It's primarily a second growth forest with a couple of lakes, a few buildings, some sporting areas and very little other development. Its setting, against the North Shore mountains, is spectacular. It is truly one of the world's great parks and so rated by those who rate these things.

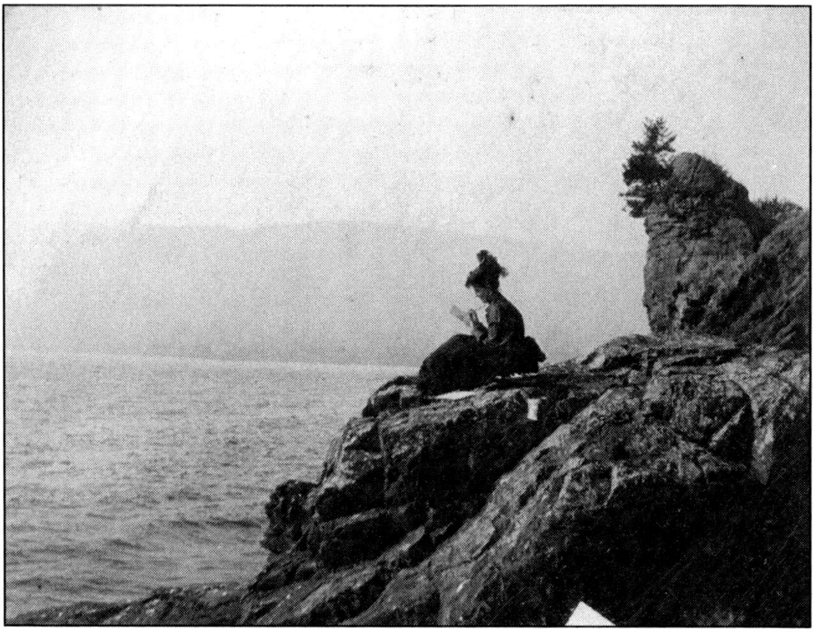

Siwash Rock.

Made Famous by poetess Pauline Johnson in Legends of Vancouver.

Photo courtesy of the City of Vancouver Archives

As this is written there is movement afoot to widen the causeway that leads to the Lions Gate Bridge to accommodate a bicycle path and, as one might expect, all hell is breaking loose. Proposals to widen it by a couple of inches have caused near riots. Stanley Park unites Vancouver as St Paul's does London and a mere look sideways at change brings, in unison, the cry—"Bugger off! And keep your hands to yourself!"—from the more polite citizens. Stanley Park, for us Lotuslanders, is sacred ground. I once opined on air, tongue in cheek, that we should open up Stanley Park like Hampstead Heath and Kensington Gardens in London and I genuinely feared for my life.

In those days when I was growing up, that had occasional winters, Lost Lagoon, a freshwater lake at the entrance of the park, sometimes froze and the skaters would last until the weather warmed to the point that a skater went through the ice, usually a couple of weeks later. Beaver Lake was also popular for skaters.

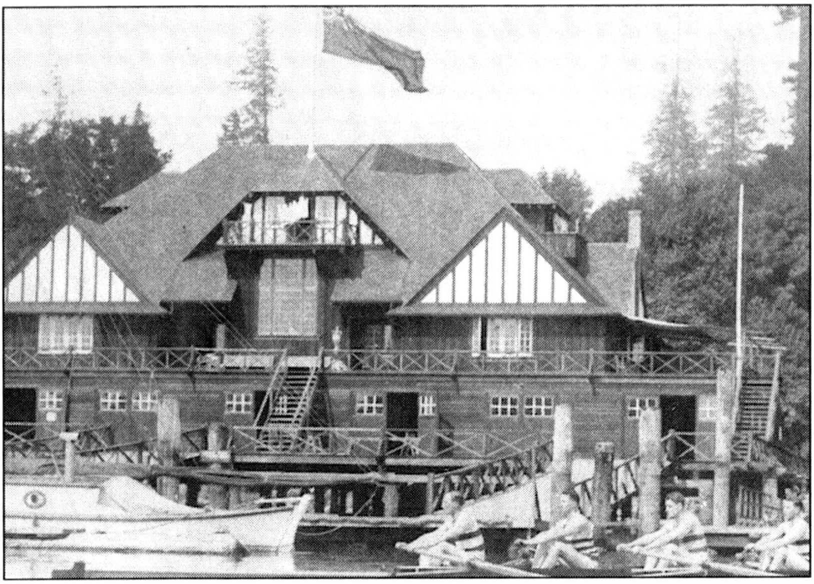

Vancouver Rowing Club.

It remains as an active club today.

Photo courtesy of the City of Vancouver Archives

The beautiful old Tudor style building on the south side as you enter the park has housed the Vancouver Rowing Club since 1898. Dad was a rower. Once, in his cups, he confided in me that he, a girl, and a mickey of gin went one night behind the Robbie Burns statue nearby and ...

Behind the Rowing Club was and remains the ever popular Malkin Bowl where Dad used to take us to Gilbert and Sullivan, which he loved. It is properly named the Marion Malkin Bowl, after the wife of W.H. Malkin, a former mayor. It is most famous for TUTS, Theatre Under The Stars, and is still going strong.

Although the main park has changed very little, the park use itself was a little different when I was a child. For one thing there was a zoo with bear cages. I especially remember a large bear, who, according to my parents, was given to us by the Russian government, improbably called Trotsky. Improbable because the human Trotsky was definitely on the outs with the boss man, Stalin, who had him murdered in Mexico in 1940. I was never happy with this story and recently got what really happened from the Vancouver Archives ...

> *"Back in 1918-1919, Canadian and other allied forces were getting a head start on the Cold War by fighting the Reds in Siberia. They withdrew in 1919 and brought back this enormous bear as a souvenir for the Stanley Park zoo. Naturally it was named Trotsky, and for 20 years the good-natured beast charmed park visitors as the zoo's most popular attraction. At 520+ pounds, the great Russian bear was thought to be the largest in captivity. As a sign of his*

popularity, Trotsky's death in 1939 made the New York Times."

In latter days, Trotsky (the bear, that is) was a rather dishevelled old-looking animal (come to think of it, so was the real Trotsky) who seemed to be so sad—which, undoubtedly, with good reason, he was. He was much loved, however. He liked peanuts and as a little boy I loved to accommodate him.

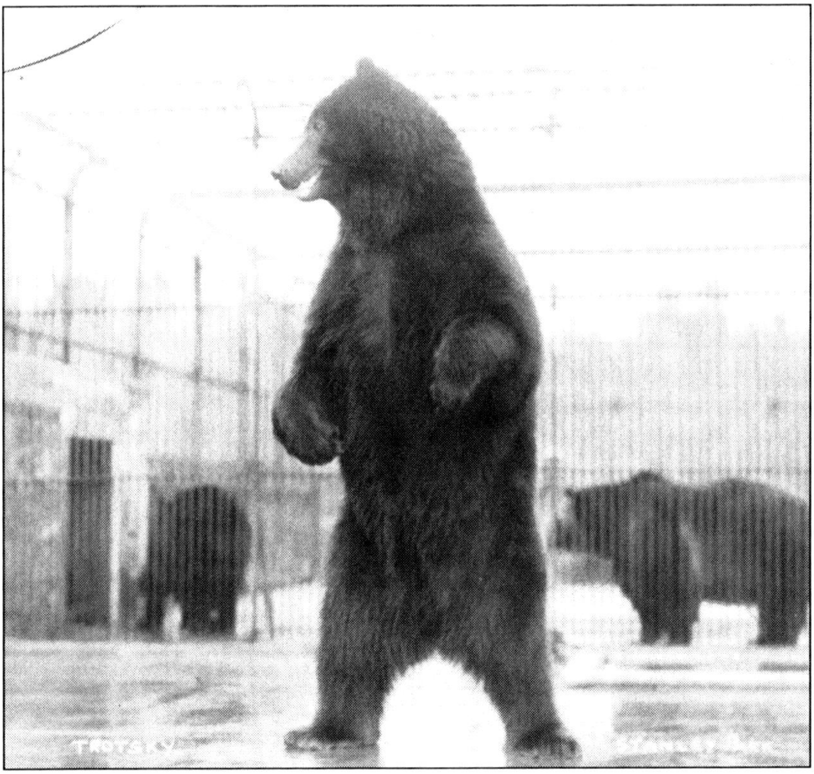

Trotsky.

Beloved and always remembered by the kids, of which I was one.

Photo courtesy of the City of Vancouver Archives

When I discovered Trotsky's picture, I also discovered a hell of a lot of people who remembered him and begged me for a copy. Bearing in mind that he died in 1939, this is remarkable. He obviously touched the hearts of a lot of little kids and proved that he was more than just your average bear.

Nearby was a polar bear cage with several at one time. The zoo closed completely in December 1997 after the last remaining animal, a polar bear named Tuk, died at age thirty-six. If anything, he looked unhappier than Trotsky. He also liked peanuts but not as much as Trotsky did. Mercifully, people came to their senses, a referendum was held, Stanley Park got rid of the zoo, and the bears and other animals stayed in the wild where they belong.

There was a monkey house and I delighted in watching them scratch themselves and scratch each other. It seemed like a lot of fun as they swung from trapeze to trapeze in search of somebody to scratch. They were also big on peanuts.

There was no aquarium but there were seals whose delightful play excited us kids especially since we were familiar with them in the wild. And there were otters who were more fun than seals as they seemed to play to their audience—us. And there were penguins. They lasted until the '70s or '80s.

You could see buffalo (North American bison) if you went to what's now the Royal Vancouver Yacht Club parking lot. There were, as I recall, three of them, mangy, and so out of place, there being no other animals around. I'm damned if I know why they were there, although there had apparently been bison in the park since 1908, and I haven't the faintest idea where they went.

The oldest manmade landmark in the park is an 1816 naval cannon located near Brockton Point. The Nine O'Clock Gun, as it is known, was first fired in 1898, and has continued to do so since. The cannon was originally detonated with a stick of dynamite, but is now activated automatically with an electronic trigger. Brockton Point, with its pretty little lighthouse built over 100 years ago, hasn't changed. It undoubtedly is the place to get the best view of the harbour, Lions Gate Bridge, and the mountains.

At Lumberman's Arch—it was rectangular then—there was a saltwater swimming pool where the *Vancouver Sun* sponsored swimming lessons for kids. The pool was closed in 1987. The area around Lumberman's Arch has always been a favourite picnic area.

I should say here that there were still some private houses in the park and a first class book, on not only the buildings but also the history of the park, is *Stanley Park's Secrets*, by Jean Barman who also authored the marvellous history of BC called *The West Beyond The West*.

Prospect Point, not far from the site of Siwash Rock, was an excellent place to watch the ocean liners pass where the Lions Gate Bridge is now. There were the classy CPR vessels, such as the *Empress of Japan*, the *Empress of Asia*, the *Empress of Canada*, and the *Empress of Britain*, which went off to faraway places, particularly the Far East. All these wonderful liners, converted into troop ships, were sunk during the war. Smaller versions plied between Vancouver and both Nanaimo and Victoria, with a midnight sailing to the latter very popular. After the war, P & O liners came from Australia and New Zealand. You could also watch the Union

Steamship vessels that plied our coast. Some of them were miniature liners—I think of the *Lady Cecilia*, the *Lady Cynthia*, and the *Lady Alexandra*. Union Steamships did a midnight return trip from Vancouver to Snug Cove, Bowen Island, lovingly called "The Booze Cruise".

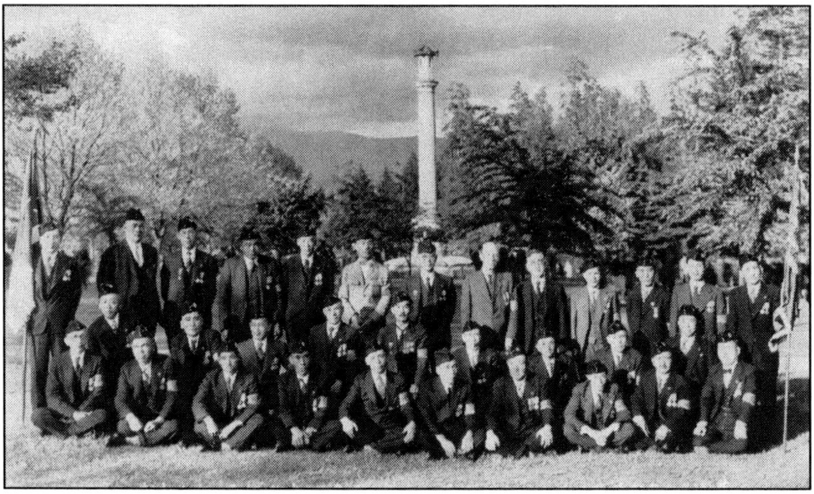

Japanese Canadian War Memorial.

Symbol of pride and shame.

Photo courtesy of Lieutenant-Colonel Roy Kawamoto, Kelowna, BC.

Ferguson Point was seen as an important lookout during the wars to ensure the safety of the city of Vancouver. Its clear vantage point is its biggest draw, offering a sweeping view of Point Grey, West Vancouver, and most notably, English Bay.

At Ferguson Point you could almost drive through the trunk of what had once been an enormous Douglas Fir—only the bottom bit remains. The walk to Beaver Lake was popular and back then you could hire a rowboat on Lost Lagoon. The Parks Board decided that too many people molested the birds so they got rid of the boats.

On Saturday afternoons in season, cousin Hugh and I would accompany our parents to Brockton Point where our fathers played cricket. As one might imagine with cricket, there was a caste system that had the "better" teams playing on Upper Brockton, "lesser" ones, like the Wednesday League (stores back then all closed on Wednesday afternoon spawning a Wednesday cricket league) played down the steep hill on Lower Brockton. Dad's team played on Upper Brockton for the Brockton Point Cricket Club.

Lower Brockton was also for juniors and contains for me a horrible memory. I was about thirteen, captain and best batsman for the St George's third XI. We were playing Shawnigan Lake and I was first in. As I went in, Captain Robinson, our coach, reminded me to "play my eye in" by patting back the first few balls. John Pearkes, son of one-time Lieutenant-Governor General George Pearkes, VC, was the bowler and when his first delivery came I swung for the boundary, missed, and was bowled for a duck. I was a chump and the stares from my teammates magnified a day-long humiliation that, obviously, I've not forgotten to this day.

My dad was a New Zealander, accounting for his attachment to the game, which, not so unusual for Vancouver kids then as now, he had played as a boy. I became fond of the game myself at St George's School during the war and my boyhood sports hero was Aussie Donald (later Sir Donald) Bradman, probably the greatest batsman of all time. My hero came to Vancouver in 1932—I was obviously too young to be there—as part of the Australian team off to England to play for "The Ashes", which were symbolic of the annual "Test Match" between the two nations.

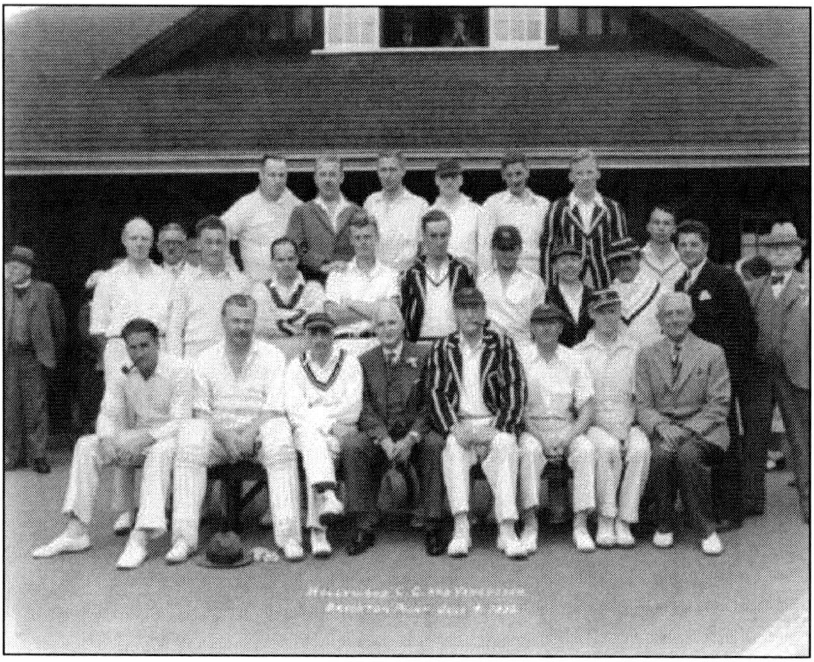

Hollywood Cricket Club and locals at Brockton Point Pavilion.

Left front, Errol Flynn; Centre Front, in ribbon coat, founder and test player, Sir C. Aubrey Smith.

Photo courtesy of the City of Vancouver Archives

The term "Ashes" came about when, in 1882, playing at the Oval in London, Australia beat England for the first time and an English writer took the bails from the wickets, burned them, and sent them to his editor saying, "Here are the ashes of English cricket." Thereafter, the "Ashes" became the annual prize. In

Don Bradman's final at bat in a "Test" played at Old Trafford in Manchester, he needed but four runs for a lifetime. The "Test" average of a century was 100 runs, a truly staggering record. You guessed it—he was bowled "for a duck", namely zilch, and had to settle for ninety-nine-point-something. I would have lobbed him something underhand rather than being the bowler that deprived the great Bradman of his century average but I guess it's like a no-hitter in baseball; the other team doesn't want to be the victim. Still ...

In 1932, the Aussies played an exhibition game at Brockton Point, which Bradman declared had the most beautiful setting of any cricket pitch he had ever played. The British Columbia lads won by ninety-eight runs, the only loss the Australians sustained on their North American tour. Cricket, like baseball, has spawned a writing culture with truly great writers involved.

Hugh and I used to go to the nearby beach and wade over to what was then Deadman Island, later HMCS Discovery. I well remember one time we misjudged the tide and came back to the cricket game sopping wet to the considerable disapproval of my mom and my Auntie Boo.

One of the great features of Stanley Park is the sea wall by which one can walk around, on the ocean, the entire park. Stanley Park had it all for kids and adults as well and no doubt, still does.

KINGS, AND QUEENS, AND FERRIES, AND CREEKS

Shaking hands with the Queen of England was a long way from being forced to sit in the coloured section of the bus going into downtown Wilmington, North Carolina.
– Althea Gibson, tennis great

I recall life before the Lions Gate Bridge, officially opened by King George VI and Queen Elizabeth in May 1939 though it was operational a year earlier. Prior to its opening, West Vancouver was serviced by small passenger-only ferries. To drive across meant the ferry from downtown Vancouver to North Vancouver, roughly where the Seabus now goes, or driving and crossing on the train bridge at the Second Narrows, next to where the Ironworkers Bridge is now. That bridge is still there. When Lions Gate was being built, my father and a number of friends, no doubt with a libation or two as fortifiers, walked across the catwalk. My mother, needless to say, was horrified.

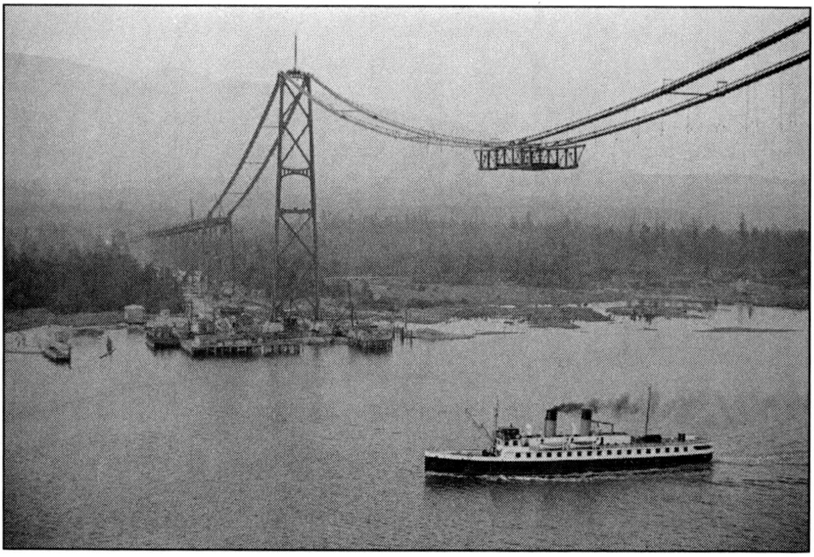

Lions Gate Bridge.

Photo courtesy of the City of Vancouver Archives, photographer James Crookall

Speaking of the King and Queen, their visit was a time of great patriotic excitement in a city that was still mostly British. Moreover, war was obviously coming and it was time to rally the colonies. They were coming to visit! Us!!! On the big day, Hugh and I stood on W41st Ave and Marguerite, waiting for the Royal limousine. We somehow had found some medals—God knows where since nobody in our family had heard a shot fired in anger for 100 years—and were excited to think that the Royal couple might notice us. Well, it was all we could do to notice them as they sped by at about thirty mph! Considering all the hype, it was a huge disappointment to us.

I remember that my dad, at Davies Paper Box, made some cardboard periscopes to help the spectators see the Royal couple. Hugh and I contemptuously rejected this assistance, wanting to see the King and Queen in person, not their reflection. In all events, we did get the war!

Speaking of the North Vancouver ferries, they transported shipyard workers from Vancouver to North Vancouver shipyards and back during the war. The workers made the immense wage for the time of one dollar per hour and when the shift ended in North Vancouver, they flew onto the boat and, within seconds, crap games developed all over the decks!

Hugh and I, along with other St George's pals, used to take the ferry on a Saturday to explore one of the North Shore rivers, the Capilano, the Lynn, or the Seymour. We would pack lunches and have a free wheeling time that is, sad to say, no longer open to kids in these safety conscious days.

It's amazing what we did—things that would have horrified our parents had they known. For example, there's a spot on Lynn Creek, now out of bounds to anyone because it is so dangerous, where we used to swing on a rope across the river and never thought anything about it. Mercifully, none of us was ever hurt. Somehow, in those days, there was a special kids' god who looked after us while we did dangerous things including hitchhiking wherever we went, girls as well as boys. For another example, most parents now forbid their children to play with firecrackers and there are strict rules about selling them to kids. For us, no such rules existed and we bought fireworks, including skyrockets and Roman Candles, to our hearts content, using them for war games! There was a Special God!

Halloween was a horrible night back in those days right through the war until about 1948 or so—now thankfully gone, being then a night of massive destruction by teenagers, who knocked over fences, turned over cars, and set things on fire. The police were out in full force and it was a night from hell. Eventually it was curtailed by the enforcement of a curfew.

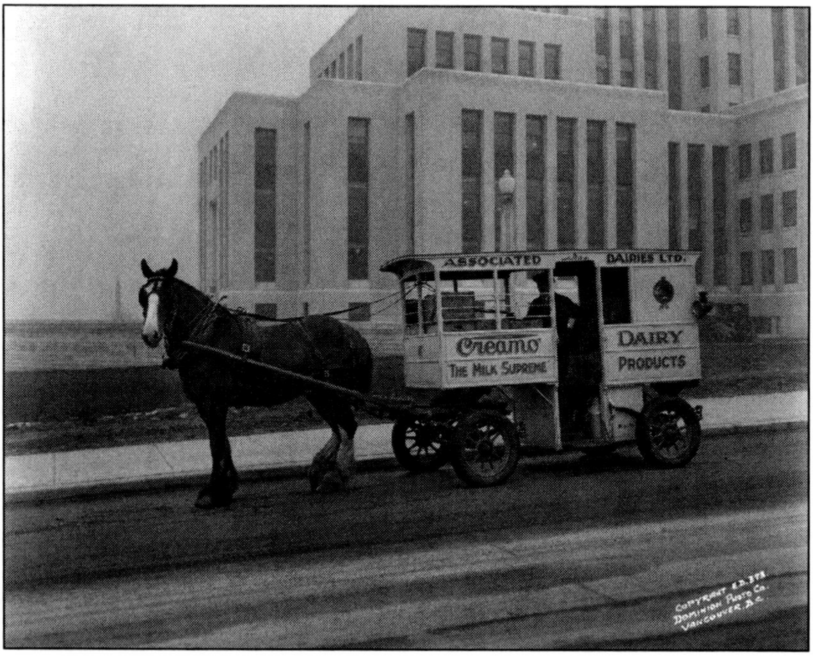

Manufacturer of Horsebuns in front of new and still City Hall 'The House That Gerry Built'

GERRY MCGEER

I can run on a laundry ticket and beat these political bums anytime.

– Fiorello Laguardia, former Mayor of New York

Mayor Gerry McGeer was a Vancouver institution and there has never been a Vancouver politician like him, before or since. He was truly beloved.

His son Mike, a lawyer who practiced in the same building where I did my articles, used to regale us with stories of Gerry on the campaign trail. One of his favourite manoeuvres was to refrain from paying his bills for about three months before the election. Then, with about a week to go, he would fill his pockets with cash and go from place to place on a Saturday, when there would be lots of people, and with a great flourish and broad Irish grin pay his bill to the great entertainment of the customers and contentment of the proprietor.

McGeer is best remembered for building the City Hall in

the middle of the Great Depression, the same one in use today. McGeer was also an MP and a senator and took some time off from city politics. He is famous for observing that while it is only 2,500 miles from Vancouver to Ottawa, it's 25,000 miles from Ottawa to Vancouver.

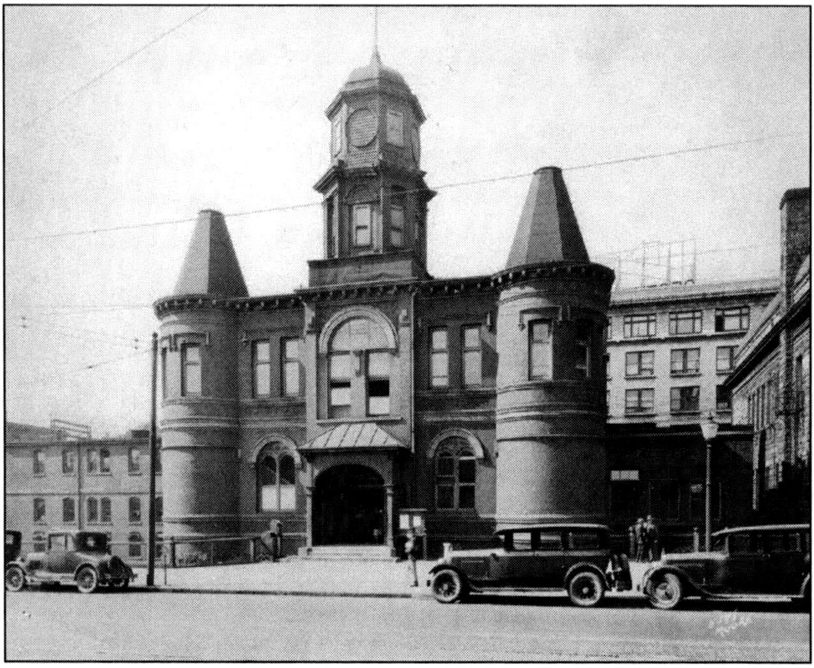

Old City Hall.

The lost art of buildings with character.

Photo courtesy of the City of Vancouver Archives, photographer W. J. Moore

When he returned in 1947 to seek re-election to City Hall, his only slogan was "Gerry's back" and he won in a landslide. Sadly, he died shortly after the election to the great sorrow of all he had served, and amused, for so many years. I was fortunate enough to sit in the BC Cabinet for five years with his nephew, Dr. Patrick McGeer, a famous BC scientist.

I remember Mayor Gerry McGeer because at the Silver Jubilee of King George V in 1935, McGeer rode through the streets in an open car and tossed toffee suckers to all of the kids. Kids don't forget mayors like that!

AND GUESS WHAT REARED ITS UGLY HEAD?

What's funny about sex? What isn't! Everything's funny about sex: the procedure, how to get it, when do you stop. It's the hidden thing … it's funnier than farts.

– Mike Wilmot, Canadian Comedian

As we aged, our bodies changed and hormones began to hop. My mother used to talk about sex in terms of it "raising its ugly head", a sign of the times. It's not that there wasn't lots of sex those days—there has been since Adam and Eve—just that after the Roaring '20s, people became more reserved in how they spoke of it. For children, it was a taboo subject, although of course there was the traditional playing doctor or some variation thereof.

Eventually, the time arrived when you must learn about the "birds and the bees" and it came for me and my classmates at St George's School when I was in my fourteenth year and about to be confirmed in the Anglican faith. Part of the confirmation process, apparently, was that we learn all about life.

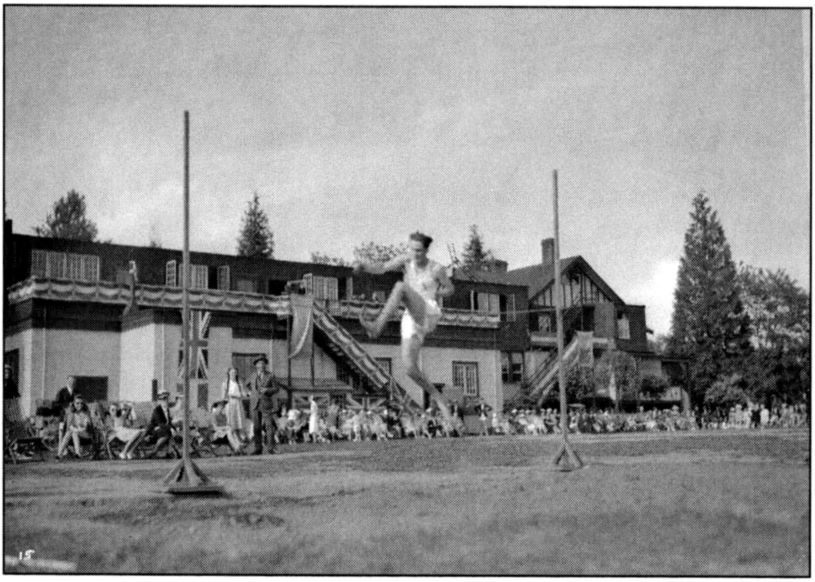

St Georges School for boys 1940.

A love hate relationship- at best!

I must say there wasn't much about the physical part of sex that we didn't understand. There was, you see, the dirt road next to the playing field at St George's where on Monday mornings there would be French safes, as we called them then, strewn all along the road. The older boys had long since explained these rubber tubes to us in full detail. One morning, one of my mates, for the devilment of it, asked a master what they were and he blushingly replied that he didn't know! Didn't know? This grown man didn't know what a contraceptive was? We sure as hell knew! But that was the attitude of the times.

Around this time an appalling bit of typical private school hypocrisy occurred when three boarders, about thirteen or fourteen, were caught masturbating and were expelled. Expelled! Can you bloody well imagine? That lifetime emotional scar for jacking off!

A master was delegated to have a little talk with us and we were, with suitable solemnity, informed that masturbation was "unmanly" and that all sorts of problems would develop to our eyesight, etc., if we indulged in this ghastly habit. That word, "unmanly", sticks in my mind and was commonly used by masters when referring to boys who weren't sporting types. Evidently, we were to believe that the headmaster and all the other masters had never played with themselves. It was a disgrace all right but it wasn't the boys who should have been ashamed. Back to our sex talk ...

I was duly summoned to the headmaster's office along with several of my mates. I went first and there was Mr. Harker sitting solemnly at his desk. He beckoned me to sit down in the soft chair in front of him, the same chair one bent over when getting the cane.

"Mair," he said, "I don't suppose you know much about sex?"

"No, sir," I replied, lying through my teeth.

Harker then mumbled something about the Latin word "semen", meaning "seed", and how the male of the species planted a "seed" inside the female and that's what it was all about.

"Mair," he asked, "do you understand?"

I replied, "Yes sir."

He then said, "Thank you, Mair, you may go, please send Rolfe in next."

That was how I learned all about sex!

NOW THE PRACTICAL PART

Grant me chastity and continence, but not yet.
– Augustine of Hippo, Confessions

It is one of the superstitions of the human mind to have imagined that virginity could be a virtue.
– Voltaire

When I was sprung from St George's in 1946, in my fifteenth year, I went to Prince of Wales High School as I have mentioned before, which was nice and coeducational. I then met lots of girls and, of course, began to date. Until then I had to be satisfied with crushes on the girls from the nearby Convent of the Sacred Heart who rode on the streetcar with us.

At PW, most of us boys were pretty horny most of the time as teenage boys tend to be. We knew, however, that if we went "all the way" we risked a pregnant girlfriend. They knew that even better!

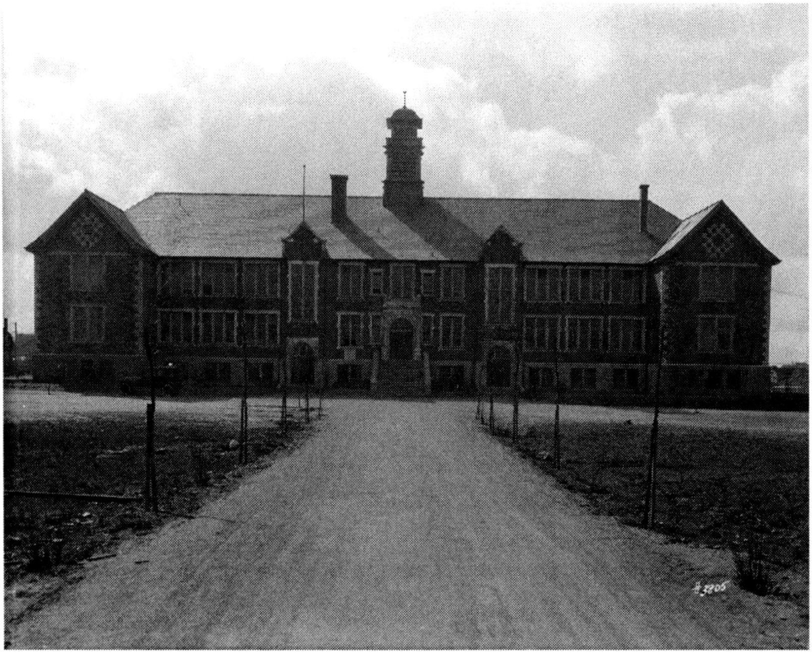

Prince of Wales High 1920.

Unchanged when I graduated in 1949. Now Shaughnessy Elementary.

With some girls you could "neck", meaning hands were permitted only above the waist, known as "feeling her up". If the young lady was less inhibited, one could "pet", which meant below the waist, but hands only. In rare but jolly cases, oral sex was the outlet. Sometimes, not often, the exercise went "all the way".

Contraceptives were just not on—pardon the pun—because either the boy was too embarrassed to buy them or he was afraid to carry them lest the girl say, "You knew you were going to do this, didn't you?" Or perhaps, "Do you use these on other girls?" Usually one used the "withdrawal method" to prevent contraception, not a very satisfactory or effective method.

I don't intend spending time on my own experiences—let me just say that I lost my virginity when I was sixteen and we continued our affair for several months, withdrawal method, and, may the saints be praised, no pregnancy ensued. I remained lucky.

It was very difficult to get a lass to go "all the way" given the dangers, accounting, I think, for the custom of early marriages and, no doubt, inconvenient pregnancies. Then, a dramatic event occurred in my early twenties, after I was married, naturally. The "pill" was discovered, placed on the market in 1961, and society changed overnight; suddenly all restrictions were off and young ladies could have as much sex as they wished. The absurd male notion that women didn't care all that much for sex was quickly and gloriously dispelled! I well remember a hooker in the West End complaining in the press that business was terrible because, since the "pill", there were so many enthusiastic amateurs! The habit amongst young ladies in the West End was that the 9 O'Clock Gun going off in Stanley Park was the signal to take their birth control pill.

This is not the place for a social discourse—suffice it to say that, in my view, the sexual and other liberation of women was the most important social happening in the twentieth century.

ZOOT SUITS AND SAILOR SUITS

Clothes make the man. Naked people have little or no influence on society.
– Mark Twain

By 1943, Vancouver Harbour was filled with vessels, especially from the United States and Great Britain. We were graced with the visit of the Cunard Line *Queen Elizabeth*, then the largest ship in the world, and being used as a troopship. The coming of the *QEI* was a huge secret, which somehow attracted about 300,000 Vancouverites, including my parents and me, lining the shores of Spanish Banks.

My father used to entertain the officers from the Royal Navy "flattops" (small Aircraft Carriers) so that I had the pleasure of meeting a great many British sailors. My father, as he often did when English people were about, instantly acquired an English accent, and such phrases as "cheerio" leapt from his tongue! This really annoyed my mother and embarrassed me.

Along with the sailors, especially the merchant seamen, came the zoot suiter. The "zoot suit" was a fad that spread from the United States to Canada and was fashionable among some young males. It consisted of a pair of baggy pants, which came up well above the waist, were wide at the knees, and tight around the ankles, and a long jacket with grotesquely wide padded shoulders. The genuine zoot suiter wore a wide-brimmed hat with a flashy hatband, and a long watch chain. In 1943 and 1944, zoot suiters often battled with servicemen (mainly sailors). Despite evidence to the contrary, sailors and the press often claimed zoot suiters were draft dodgers—"slackers" in common parlance—thumbing their noses at heroic servicemen by loafing about on street corners causing trouble.

As in other cities with zoot suiter dustups with servicemen, the defiance expressed by wearing the suits was little more than just symbolic. But just as wearing a hoodie today doesn't mean you're a hooligan, draped pants and zoot-esque suits were simply in style. Styles of the young invariably piss off their elders and the zoot suit was no exception. Chinatown was the place for young hipsters to buy their clothes. I remember On Wo tailors as one popular source. The fad spread to the west side of the city where young lads adopted the pants style with the knee at twenty-eight inches and the ankle at sixteen. They didn't, for the most part however, adopt the jacket, the hat, or the watch-chain.

I remember when a bunch of us went down to Stanley Park to

witness a fight and I must say it wasn't much. There were far more bystanders than fighters. Generally speaking, the press made far too much of it all, calling them the Zoot Suit Riots, which they clearly weren't, and really the whole issue was no more than a few fights of little lasting consequence. Meanwhile, in Montreal, where confrontations became French-English fights, it was a much more serious matter and "riots" was a more appropriate term.

The zoot suit certainly got the local adults' knickers in a knot. They saw Vancouver's youth sending a message to the rest of the world that they were slackers and bums that beat up valiant visiting servicemen—a rather typical adult approach to a teenage phenomenon they didn't understand.

Like all fads, the zoot suit faded and was soon forgotten.

GAMES WE PLAYED AND WATCHED

People ask me what I do in winter when there's no baseball. I'll tell you what I do. I stare out the window and wait for spring.
– Rogers Hornsby, Hall of Famer extraordinaire

During my childhood and early teens, the only professional sports in Vancouver were lacrosse and baseball, the latter played at Athletic Park at 5th and Hemlock near where the south end of the Granville Bridge is now. (I'll talk of hockey in a moment.)

Our team was the Vancouver Capilanos, owned by Sick's Breweries, and while they were in a Class D league (it would be classed no worse than AA today), they played exciting baseball. (In those days you couldn't advertise booze and Sick's Capilano was a popular beer—pretty slick, huh?) There were the Tran brothers, Ray and Len, Frank Mullins our big hitter, Bill Brenner our catcher and a heavy hitter, pitcher Dewey Soriano, Jimmy

Estrada, whose forte was fouling off pitches until he took a walk. Vancouver has always been a good baseball town and, in my view, with a decent park would easily sustain a major league team. BC Place Stadium held an exhibition game about twenty-five years ago between two major league teams and I was there as a guest of the late Senator Ray Perrault who was labouring very hard to get Major League ball for Vancouver. The only problem was that you couldn't see the ball! I told Ray that I didn't think that Vancouver was ready for pantomime baseball. I wonder if that problem at BC Place Stadium has been rectified!

Baseball was, and very much remains, my favourite game. Amongst its other virtues, a marvellous literature has grown up about the game and I couldn't get enough of it and still can't. The Victoria team had, at third, Gil McDougald, later a star with the (ugh!) Yankees. It wasn't Major League but it was baseball and the Caps were our team.

Probably the most famous game played at Athletic Park was in October 1934, when, in a blinding rainstorm, the barnstorming New York Yankees, led by Babe Ruth, on their way to Japan, played a local group—and thrashed them. The Yankees and their manager, Joe McCarthy, didn't want to play but the Bambino said, "If these good folks came to watch us we owe them a game. Let's go!"

Most kids had favourite major-league teams and would argue about them at great length. I was a Brooklyn Dodger fan and a number of my friends were New York Giant or St Louis Cardinal fans. Then of course there were the Yankee fans that came out at World Series time and annoyed the hell out of us because the Yankees invariably won.

Football was High School, Junior, and UBC. For spectators, Vancouver College, then and now a Catholic High School for boys, was all the rage. Their home field was also Athletic Park and they played American football rather than Canadian, their opponents being high schools from the Seattle area plus one from Hawaii whose kicker kicked barefoot. They would pack the park on a Friday night and did well. An amusing story involved their star fullback Bob Murphy. Some dozen US Catholic colleges approached him with scholarship offers assuming with that surname and attending a Catholic school that Bob was Catholic. He wasn't.

The "Fighting Irish", as they were called, even had a Bowl Game, the "Evergreen Bowl". Cousin Ann's future husband and great friend of mine, the late Clark Robertson, played for "The College".

Junior football was mostly played on local parks so that the spectators were limited unless it was a Western Final game, often it seemed, involving the Vancouver Blue Bombers coached by an Indo-Canadian, Ranji Mattu, in which case it was played at Varsity Stadium at UBC before a large crowd. UBC itself always had such lousy teams that, apart from a few faithful students, it couldn't draw flies. It's interesting to note that information on Ranji Mattu is very difficult to obtain. When one goes to the Internet the only information relates to documents at the University of British Columbia. Since there is a coveted trophy named after Mattu one has to wonder if there is a touch of racism here. He was an extraordinarily successful coach yet while we remember his players well, not him.

Rugby was a popular participant sport as it is today. Again it was mostly played on local parks but the Oval at Brockton Point in Stanley Park was the site of important league games and league finals.

Soccer was moderately popular, especially in schools where parents liked it because the equipment wasn't expensive and, like Rugby, serious injuries were rare. There was a senior league whose better teams often played exhibitions with English and Scottish teams.

Hockey was very popular, with the Vancouver Canucks, an amateur team, playing in the Pacific Coast League. While I say amateur, the better word is "shamateur" as players were paid. They won the "World Amateur" title in 1946 beating the Boston Olympics. They played at the old Forum on the PNE grounds and morphed into the Canucks of the WHL and later the NHL. We all had NHL favourites.

When I was a boy, the only hockey was on CBC radio from Maple Leaf Gardens. Apart from the one time a year the Montreal Canadiens played in Toronto on a Saturday Night, it was Toronto all season long. CBC had decided, no doubt accompanied by political pressure, that all people outside of Quebec should be Leaf fans. I wasn't and no bluddy radio was going to tell me who to cheer for.

The announcer was the sainted (in Toronto) Foster Hewitt and was he ever a homer! Between periods was The Hot Stove

League, which was openly anti-Canadiens and Quebeckers of the French persuasion; Hewitt prattled on, devoted to the Leafs and patronizing, at best, to all other teams. All right-minded little boys in the hinterland must grow up as sturdy Leaf fans.

I was, even at that age, a contrarian, and began pulling for the Habs. When anyone beat them I grieved, but when it was at the hands of the Leafs, it was as bad as your girlfriend breaking up with you.

In the 1947 Stanley Cup the Leafs did just that, with Maurice "Rocket" Richard being tossed out of the Series for getting into a stick fight with a journeyman named Bill Eziniki. Richard received such a harsh penalty because the Leafs owner, Conn Smyth, a bitter Francophobe, was a power in the league and demanded it.

Shortly after this disaster, my father brought home a Leafs program with all the Leaf autographs on it from a Toronto business trip. He was sure I would be thrilled to death! I sure as hell wasn't but I didn't know what to do since I didn't want to hurt my Dad's feelings. I put on a brave face but evidently not brave enough for many years later, having a drink with him on our boat, he had learned that I was a Habs fan and asked if that was what made my attitude about the Leafs program so tepid, to put it mildly.

My Dad was a cricketer and knew nothing about hockey except that people in Western Canada were, so his Toronto friends told him, all Leaf fans. A visit to a Canucks game when the Canadiens are playing soon puts paid to that typical Ontario crap.

My allegiance to the Habs paid off. My best night was the Stanley Cup final game in 1960 when the Habs beat the Leafs in four straight, the last game 4-0, with "The Rocket" getting the last goal. He knew, though we didn't, that this was his last as he dove into the net to get the puck. I am a Vancouver boy, born and bred, and I'm a loyal Canucks fan ... except when the Habs score a goal against us, a little cheer goes up deep inside me. It's all so different now—but man oh man it was fun to be a Habs fan in their glory years.

Golf was popular and in 1936 a major PGA tournament, the Jubilee Open, was held at the old Shaughnessy course in honour of Vancouver's fiftieth birthday. It was won by a local boy, amateur Ken Black, whose Dad was Davie Black, the long time pro at Shaughnessy. All the better pros from the US were there and Ken was the toast of the town. During the war, Byron Nelson and "Jug" McSpadden toured North America, and on one occasion played at Quilchena Golf Club, the old course, and my dad took me. McSpadden was no match for Nelson who was probably the best in the world although most of the great players like Ben Hogan, Sam Snead, and Lloyd Mangrum were in the Services. I saw another exhibition by Nelson in the early '50s playing in a foursome that included the great Stan Leonard, Ernie Brown from Quilchena, a good friend of mine as I grew older, and Leroy Goldsworthy, the pro at Point Grey where the match was played. Nelson was magnificent though clearly past his prime, a true gentleman with a fine swing and a virtually flawless game. (Point Grey was where I caddied during the war and another expatriate Scot, Dunc Sutherland, was the pro. The players gave the caddie money to Dunc who then gave it to the caddie. I had reason to believe the cheap bastard withheld any tips!) The great woman pro, Mildred "Babe" Didrikson Zaharias played an exhibition at Shaughnessy about 1950 and her playing partners were Stan Leonard, Jock MacKinnon from Capilano, and the home pro, Fred Wood. On the eleventh—I was there and heard it—Jock MacKinnon, in his Scots brogue, said, "Ah, Babe, ye out drove me again" to which the Babe replied, "You're easy, Jock." Another popular American pro to hold exhibitions in Vancouver during this period was Ed "Porky" Oliver.

Box Lacrosse had its fans and very loyal ones they were. They still are, I'm told. It was really the only major league sport in that the winner of the local league, often the New Westminster Salmonbellies or the Vancouver Burrards it seemed, played for the national championship. I hate to admit that I have never seen a lacrosse game, field or box, in my life and, of course, never played the game.

Vancouver was quite a British City so Cricket had a special popularity. It was not only played at Brockton Point but also on several other parks around the city with half a dozen or more regular teams. The private schools played cricket and we were taught at St George's that cricket was the civilizing factor in the British Empire. I suppose it was when you consider its influence in Australia, New Zealand, the West Indies, India, Pakistan, Ceylon, and South Africa, which all became First Class cricket countries.

Sir Henry Newbold, the ultimate patriot poet, wrote the classic song about cricket and it was required memorizing at St George's. Here it is:

"Vitai Lampada"

There's a breathless hush in the Close to-night—
Ten to make and the match to win—
A bumping pitch and a blinding light,
An hour to play and the last man in.
And it's not for the sake of a ribboned coat,
Or the selfish hope of a season's fame,
But his Captain's hand on his shoulder smote
"Play up! play up! and play the game!"

The sand of the desert is sodden red,
Red with the wreck of a square that broke;
The Gatling's jammed and the colonel dead,
And the regiment blind with dust and smoke.
The river of death has brimmed his banks,
And England's far, and Honour a name,
But the voice of schoolboy rallies the ranks,
"Play up! play up! and play the game!"

This is the word that year by year
While in her place the School is set
Every one of her sons must hear,
And none that hears it dare forget.
This they all with a joyful mind
Bear through life like a torch in flame,
And falling fling to the host behind—
"Play up! play up! and play the game!"

THE ULTIMATE BASEBALL TREASON!

If a woman has to choose between catching a fly ball and saving an infant's life, she will choose to save the infant's life without even considering if there is a man on base.

– Dave Barry

You gotta be a man to play baseball for a living, but you gotta be a lot of little boy too.

– Roy Campanella, Hall of Fame Catcher for the Dodgers

Today is true confessions day and there will be a lot of old friends rolling in their graves when they learn what I have to say.

From the time I was a small child I was a Brooklyn Dodger fan, big time! My first recollection was the Mickey Owen dropped third strike in the 1941 World Series but my interest really was piqued in 1947 when Jackie Robinson was the first Black to play in the major leagues in the twentieth century and he played for "my team".

It was both great and terrible to be a Dodger fan during the '40s and '50s. They had a marvellous team, dubbed the Boys of Summer by Roger Kahn, and won several pennants with Jackie, Pee Wee, Gil, Billy, Campy, Carl, Gene, and the Duke, and some fine pitchers like "Oisk", Hughie, and "Newk". Unhappily, they continually lost the World Series to the Yankees, which wasn't remedied until 1955.

All through those years one of my great friends was the late Robin Heather, a golf pal, a beer drinking buddy, and a fellow history buff. Robin, or "Birdie" as we called him, was a devoted New York Giants fan. Until he and I started to fight about baseball, I had never much thought about the Giants but concentrated on the Cards as the enemy. That all changed with Robin—and Willie Mays.

Probably the worst moment in my life was 1951 when the Giants came back from 13.5 games to tie the Dodgers on the last day, then beat them in a three game playoff. The Bums would have lost on the last game of the season had not Jackie hit a homer in the bottom of the eleventh to beat the Phillies. It wasn't, of course, just the loss of the playoffs, but the way it happened. With the Dodgers leading 4-2 in the bottom of the ninth, Bobby Thompson, with two on, homered for the Giants and that was that. It would have been bad enough had I not been sitting in my car with Robin listening to the game on the radio.

It was murder, and for the rest of his life I would hear about it every time we met! The only thing I had going was when he and I were fishing, and in landing a huge trout I'd hooked, Robin blew it and knocked the fish off the line and, I can say, he never heard the end of that. But it wasn't the same and not nearly enough. (An interesting feature was that when Thompson circled the bases after his homerun, Jackie Robinson followed him the whole way to make sure he touched all the bases. The others had all quit but Robinson never did.)

In the late '50s the Giants and the Dodgers moved to San Francisco and Los Angeles respectively. I managed to maintain my allegiance and was particularly delighted in 1962 when the Dodgers beat the Yankees in four straight. Somehow, though, the rivalry with the Giants was just not the same. I no longer hated them and in fact would attend their games whenever in the Bay City. As time passed, I found that I was losing interest in my beloved Dodgers. No longer were they called "The Bums" and no longer did they have the old romanticism about them. After Sandy and Junior left, they were just like any other ball club.

Last year, in 2014, I had it. The Dodgers had the best team in the National League and beat the Giants like they owned them during the regular season. My interest was restored as it seemed a cinch I would, once more, see a Dodger World Series victory. When during mid season, I caught a game where Vin Scully, from the Brooklyn days, was the announcer, it was like I had died and gone to heaven. The old days had magically been reincarnated.

Then they blew it. These multimillionaires with their flashy cars and flashier girlfriends simply couldn't do justice to the money that had been spent on them nor to the fans who'd been so faithful. They choked and they didn't seem to care. One could almost hear that high-pitched scream from Jackie in his grave.

The San Francisco Giants, of course, won the World Series and did it in the American League park with its idiotic designated hitter rule, and did it coming back three games to two. It was a gutsy performance by a team that had no business being there.

It ate at me. This was the kind of team I have always loved. One that always tried; one that always cared, win or lose.

Here it comes ...

In early 2015, in the San Francisco airport, I marched into a sports store and bought—are you ready for this—a San Francisco Giants baseball cap, which I now regularly wear.

Birdie would chuckle but he would understand.

THEY'RE OFF!

You're better off betting on a horse than betting on a man. A horse may not be able to hold you tight, but he doesn't wanna wander from the stable at night.

– Betty Grable

In the '30s and '40s, Vancouver was a major-league horse-racing centre in North America. It had two one-mile tracks in Richmond, Brighouse and Lansdowne, both with a clay-loam base. There was another track at the PNE called Hastings Park, now Exhibition Park, but because the track at half a mile was so short with such sharp turns, it couldn't get good horses. That remains true today. This was not true of Lansdowne and Brighouse, which, with their one-mile tracks, attracted some very good horses indeed.

By the late 1940s, Brighouse had long been shut down and Lansdowne was suffering badly for lack of attendance. It was difficult for people to get to Richmond with there being no bridge, leaving a slow and inadequate ferry service. Lansdowne, in its heyday, was blessed with some very fine horses indeed. Probably the best known were owned by Major Austin C. Taylor whose stallion Indian Broom came third in the Kentucky Derby. According to his biography at the Hall of Fame, Austin Taylor *"assembled the most powerful stable ever seen in Western Canada during the 1930s. His racing stable competed in Vancouver as well as at tracks throughout California. In 1936, his horses won every handicap of importance at the Tanforan Racetrack meeting including Indian Broom who set a world record of 1:47 3/5 for a mile and an eighth on dirt. Indian Broom went on to run third in the Kentucky Derby and in his four years of racing won a number of races including the San Juan Capistrano Handicap."*

Among Austin Taylor's other successful horses: Special Agent—won the 1937 San Pasqual Handicap at Santa Anita Park, equalling the track record; Minulus—won the 1938 Santa Anita Oaks; Whichcee—wins include the 1937 San Francisco Handicap, the San Antonio Handicap, plus the inaugural running of the Los Angeles Handicap at Hollywood Park Racetrack in 1938; Colonel Mack—in 1956 won the Los Angeles Handicap and the Bing Crosby Handicap at Del Mar Racetrack.

Sadly, in the 1950s, it was decided to close down Lansdowne because of lack of crowds. This meant that Jack Diamond who owned Lansdowne and Sam Randall who owned Hastings Park got together, pooled racing days, upgraded Hastings Park to 5/8th of a mile, and it became the sole racetrack. I said sadly because shortly thereafter the Oak Street bridge was built and no doubt would have much enhanced the crowds at Lansdowne. Like many young people, I worked at Lansdowne Park and was very sad indeed to see it go. We no longer had big league horse-racing.

There have been many efforts since to get a one-mile track up and going; however, they haven't been successful mainly because of a lack of available land and decent public transit to anywhere there appeared to be land available. As a result we don't have good horses and Exhibition Park has had to resort to slot machines to try to make a go of it.

One cannot speak of horse racing in British Columbia without saying, with reverence, the name Jack Short. Here is an excerpt of a biographical sketch from the BC sports Hall of Fame:

> *"For many British Columbians, Jack Short was and will always be remembered as the voice of horse racing. For 43 seasons, Short called the races at Hastings Park, Lansdowne, Brighouse in Richmond and at The Willows, Colwood, and Sandown on Vancouver Island.*
>
> *"His love for the sport began as an eleven-year-old at the Willows track in Victoria. There he became an apprentice jockey. However, he quickly learned that God had not designed lean six-footers to perform as jockeys and he moved on to various jobs, including a porter on a steamship and a dance troupe performer.*
>
> *"In 1933 he began broadcasting results of the races at CKMO as a sound effects man banged hollowed coconut shells on a table to simulate hoof beats Short rattled off the horses' names from his notes.*
>
> *"Short could talk fast and clearly—running through a ten-*

horse field in quick, accurate succession—and he made the event so vibrant that many radio listeners were enticed to come out to see the real thing.

"When he left his perch on the roof at Sandown Park, [Victoria,] in 1976, his eye was still keen and his voice still hit the high notes, he was at the top of his game. When he said 'Adios Amigos' for the final time, he had called between 48,000 and 50,000 races, more than any track announcer in North America."

As a boy, I listened to Jack Short faithfully. When a radio station, CJOR, for whom I was then broadcasting, moved into new studios in 1983, I was privileged to interview Jack and as part of that, I asked him to call a race after giving him eight horses from my time and telling him that it would be a travesty of justice if Goldstreworth, my all-time favourite, didn't win! He called the race, Goldstreworth won in a PhotoFinish, and I was delighted, but more than that, proud as punch to have interviewed a sports hero of mine and of racing fans all over North America.

Finally, a note of interest: for many years, Harry Filion was the track photographer as well as the Senior Photographer at the *Vancouver Sun*. His daughter is the famous broadcaster and friend, Vicki Gabereau.

Horse racing has slipped in popularity with the legalization of casinos all over the continent and the growing antipathy to sports that involve animals. In its day, however, Vancouver was major league.

DOGS ... AND THE ODD CAT, WHICH IS TO SAY ALL OF THEM

Women and cats will do as they please, and men and dogs should relax and get used to the idea.

– Robert A. Heinlein

If I have any beliefs about immortality, it is that certain dogs I have known will go to heaven, and very, very few persons.

– James Thurber

Vancouver was and is a doggy town. I don't remember a day there wasn't a dog involved in my life and I can't think of many friends that didn't have a pooch.

As mentioned earlier, my first dog was an English Sheepdog named Skipper about whom I recall very little, but do remember. The first I really remember with particularity was Mandy, a black Cocker Spaniel. You probably wouldn't call a black female dog Mandy these days but to my father, a then common name for Black ladies seemed perfectly in order for a dog! Mercifully, for all, times have changed.

Mandy was a darling dog that survived distemper, leaving her with a partially paralyzed hind leg that she bore with distinctive bravery, following Denis and me on our bikes wherever we went. Denis's Airedale, Jake, able bodied, usually said the hell with it, flopped down, and slept.

Those were the days of coal furnaces and it was my job to keep the coal bin full and shovel it into the furnace. I was, it seems, the guy the Iron Fireman Company had as their logo! Mandy loved that coal bin. A few days after she died I went into the coal bin, shovel in hand, and suddenly felt as if my skin was coming off—I was covered with fleas! Evidently that happens when a dog abandons its favourite lying down spot!

We didn't get another dog until I was in my teens and Gussie, a Daschund, arrived, my first exposure to this breed. Gussie was a great little dog and a sure conversation piece when you were out walking. She loved to get under the covers at night and go right down to my feet and cheerfully, it seemed, sleep well, whereas I'm always glad I don't have to sleep next to those feet!

During my last two years at UBC, a fraternity brother, Peter Bishop, lived with us. I invited him for Christmas and he stayed for three years! Peter's story was a sad one. A brilliant student, he was born and spent his life until the end of World War II in

Vienna. After the war, his English being perfect and without accent, he translated for the US Army while attending the University of Vienna. In 1954, Peter attended the University of Pennsylvania on a full scholarship. To show that universities have mad bureaucracies too, while Peter had spent two years, with honours both years, in Vienna, Pennsylvania only credited him with one. Peter had joined my fraternity, Zeta Psi, and when his visa ran out an Elder Brother arranged a scholarship for him to attend UBC and live at the Zete House. UBC, like Pennsylvania, only granted him one year for his two years honours there!

I don't know if it was common ancestry that did it but Peter and Gussie became great pals and my abiding recollection of them was Peter sending Christmas cards by the score with Gussie licking the envelopes and stamps.

Tragically, Peter, whom everyone loved, died by his own hand after he had received his doctorate, had established himself as a professor at the University of Toronto, was married, and had a weekly radio show on International Affairs with the CBC. He was badly troubled but few, in those days, understood such things.

It's time for a cat. Around 1954, we moved to a new house and out front, by the sidewalk, was a huge rhododendron bush. We had a large Persian cat we called, for reasons you will soon learn, Tiger. Tiger used to lie in wait under the cover of the rhododendron tree and when a dog came by would leap up onto his back hanging on by his ever-sharp claws! Dogs would cross that road several houses away from that tree.

I was married and living in a tiny house in Richmond when we obtained a lovely, but very large black Labrador we called Beauregard after a character in Walt Kelly's wonderful comic satire, *Pogo*. Beauregard loved kids, which was good since we had three of them, with number four, Karen, born later. I well remember Shawn as a baby would crawl over to "Beau" and grab him by the balls! Beau would gently nudge her away from this tender spot. Ken and his friend Hughie from across the street would wrestle and if one was on top for what Beau regarded as too long, he would take him, by his belt, and gently pull him off.

Beauregard wasn't popular, however, with my dad from the day when he (Dad, that is) brought his new Mercedes out and Beau jumped up to lick my mum and scratched the paint on Dad's pride and joy—the car, that is.

Beau became too much for Eve to handle along with three, soon to be four, kids under six years old, and he wound up with a friendly farm family in the Fraser Valley.

In Christmas 1958, we bought Tacky and Tar, litter mates, who were of indeterminate ancestry; they rather resembled Skye Terriers but smaller. Tar came to an early sticky end losing a contest with a car but Tacky went on forever, finally dying at sixteen. She had a passionate hatred for all postmen (as they were then known) no matter where we lived and would wait by the mail slot so she could grab the mail and trash it!

Along the way we acquired Macgregor, sort of a border collie, who was the gentlest dog in the world—until he saw a motorcycle. He hated motorcycles and would try to remove the cyclist from his seat. The day he sent a motorcycle and rider over a neighbour's lawn and through the basement window was finis for Macgregor, who was loved by all but motorcyclists.

When we moved to Kamloops in 1969, we bought another black Lab whom we named Wallace after Governor George Wallace of Alabama, an out and out racist, thinking that naming a black dog after him might drive him into a fit of anger and hasten his departure from this life. Alas, to the best of my knowledge, Governor Wallace remained in ignorance of his namesake.

Wallace (the dog) used to come fishing with me and would sit in the bow surveying all he saw as I motored down to where I would anchor and toss a fly. Wallace would soon fall asleep and fall unceremoniously in the lake! Getting a soaking wet Labrador back into a small boat is indeed a challenge. Walking one evening with our youngest daughter, Karen, Wallace was killed by a car right before her nine-year-old eyes. It was a hard lesson on the impermanence of loved ones.

This led to Amigo, truly a cow dog. We lived on the North Thompson River and had a couple of horses. Amigo took to grasping them by the tail and getting kicked unto serious vet bills to get his ribs back in place. It was a painful experience, to Amigo and his owner's wallet, and, thankfully, he eventually learned to discontinue this hobby.

When we moved to Cherry Creek we bought, as a companion for Amigo, a black Labrador bitch who we named Kona after a Hawaiian holiday on the Big Island. (By way of aside, when we moved to the ranch, on the first day both dogs came home yipping in pain from the cactus needles they'd stepped on. Eve and I pulled them out to great howls and neither dog ever stepped on a cactus again!) We had neglected to have Kona spayed and in the summer of 1977, after Eve and I had parted, she (Kona, that is) gave birth to a double litter, one half from a purebred neighbouring Lab and, surprise, surprise, the other half by Amigo. On a visit, I saw there was one little yellow Lab pup left who was waiting to be adopted or receive an early departure from this vale of tears. I took him, named him Casey, and flew him home to Victoria (I was a cabinet minister and lived there at the time) by government plane.

Casey had but two bad habits. He loved to play with little dogs; his shtick being to pick them up by the collar and shake them. Unhappily, chances of a toy poodle surviving this merry game were rather slim. The other was he loved to escape and wander.

When I, with Patti (wife number two) and kids, moved to North Vancouver, we put a large cage in the back for Casey to stay when no one was home. Somehow he found a way to undo the latch and, like Harry Houdini, would be free in a trice. Patti got a lock for the gate, which I thought a waste of money assuming he would probably learn the combination.

We got a companion for him, a female American Cocker named Pujah. They were devoted and little Pujah ran Casey's life. When Casey would escape without Pujah, she would be waiting at the gate when we got him home and would give him a good bite on the nose.

For all his peccadilloes, Casey turned out to be a lovely guy, loved by all. When he finished his earthly stretch, we weren't going to get another dog—until two days later. We looked in the Classifieds and saw a litter of Chocolate Labs in Aldergrove and were there the next day. A cute little brown bundle came over and laid across my feet, thus Clancy came into our lives.

We had a cat, a ginger named Sesame, one tough feline who carried a hole in one ear from a tussle with a raccoon. When she saw Clancy, who rushed up with puppy-like enthusiasm to greet her, she batted him twice in the face with open claws, thus establishing the permanent pecking order!

In 1988, when Premier Bill Vander Zalm was in deep trouble, I did a bit on air, calling upon people to vote for Clancy for leader, with two rallying cries—"I fancy Clancy" and "Get a leg up in your neighbourhood, vote Clancy"—the latter slogan thanks to the PR man supreme, the late Tommy Butler, who founded the World Belly Flop and Cannonball Championship contest. We had posters made, a couple were displayed at the next Socred Annual Convention, and it was great fun. Even Bill laughed.

In 1994, a new love came to Clancy as Wendy and I moved into the house Patti and I had shared. (After Wendy and I got together in September 1993, we lived in her apartment in Abbotsford and Patti stayed in our home until she bought a condo the following February.) Clancy saw Wendy and, like his master before him, fell head over heels in love. They walked together and talked together. She was never out of his sight. He was a wonderful character and loved by all.

In 2000, Clancy was riddled with cancer. To his great chagrin, he was incontinent, and it was time to go. Like all Labs, he was courageous to a fault and on the afternoon of the terrible day, we took him across the street for a whizz and he ran like hell down into his favourite stream and splashed around as if he were a pup. Were we making a mistake? No. When he got home he collapsed. It was indeed time and the memory of hugging him as he got the needle makes me weep to this day.

We weren't going to get another dog. Too much trouble and too hard to part from. Yet every night when we would have our nightcap, we'd weep remembering how Clancy would come over to Wendy, sit down in front of her, and stare hard at the glass waiting for her to finish and give him the ice. Whether it was the ice or the taste of Scotch whiskey we'll never know. I suspect the latter!

One night, not long after Clancy had gone and it was nightcap time, I picked up a book of poetry we keep below our table top and, believe it or not, I opened at this poem by Wilfred Funk entitled "Rest In Peace":

Father in thy holy tent,
I kneel a humble suppliant
A dog has died today on earth
Of little worth
Yet very dear

Gather him in thine arms
If only for awhile

I fear he will be lonely
Shield him with thy smile.

What a chance choice! The tears flowed and the next day, thanks to our good friend and dog trainer, Ann Jackson, who was a regular on my show, we found a breeder who had a Labrador bitch coming into heat. Arrangements were made with Agneta and Willie at Big Valley Labradors for us to have first dibs on a male chocolate—it turned out there were six blacks, and two chocolate, and that all but one of the eight surviving pups were female. The lone male, happily, was chocolate. Thus, "Big Valley's Chauncey of Deveron" came to Lions Bay.

Upon entering the front door, at ten weeks old, he darted under my computer and pulled out all the wires! In fact, he turned out not to be a destructive puppy as Labs often are. He was a wonderful dog who quickly and emphatically demonstrated why Labs are called retrievers.

Chauncey was just twelve weeks old when, on a bitterly cold January morning, we took him to the beach. I suggested we throw him a stick and Wendy said it's too cold and he's too young. I said, let him make the decision. I threw a piece of bark into the water about twenty-five feet away and Chauncey charged in after it. When his feet didn't touch the ground he turned around, anxiously, then turned back, got the bark, and dropped it on my feet and stood there, head slanted, grinning from ear to ear! He was a swimmer, as well as a retriever, all right! Chauncey went to the beach for his swim every day and the only thing he enjoyed more than swimming was swimming in the teeming rain!

Like all Labs, Chauncey was as gentle as a lamb—until, that is, he sensed one of his family was threatened. One morning he and I were coming back from the beach when he saw a bear on a lawn about fifty metres away. He tore the leash out of my hand, chased that bear across the busy Sea-to-Sky Highway and up into a nearby woods. I was sure that was the end of our gallant pooch but he came back half an hour later, tail going a mile a minute, and wreathed in smiles. I was his family and that was his job.

It's interesting, I think, that Chauncey and seals got along fine. Quite often seals came up while he was retrieving his tennis ball—often right beside him—and both took the meeting quite casually. One morning Wendy catapulted his tennis ball into the water and before Chauncey could get to it, a seal came up and grabbed it! We could hardly believe our eyes! Chauncey swam around and around for at least five minutes looking for it before coming ashore thinking, I suppose, that the seal was playing a game with him!

At nightcap time Chauncey had a different shtick than Clancy—he had his stuffed "Duck", which he took wherever he went in the house, like Linus and his blanket. Instead of ice, he demanded that "Duck" be tossed into the kitchen so he could retrieve it.

As you may have surmised, Chauncey played a huge role in our lives. I believe that in addition to loving Wendy and me very much, he was a conduit that transmitted love between us. Unhappily, dogs don't live long—but the consolation is that they live in our hearts forever and we lost our pal in August 2013. We won't get another unless and until my health permits.

Chauncey died with his boots on. He had, at twelve, a serious breathing problem and he was to take it easy—advice much easier said than done!

Jack Bilideau, the wonderful guy who services our hot tub every week, is a dog man. He was Chauncey's best pal and when we were away, Chauncey stayed with Jack and his two Dobermans. On the day in question in August 2013, Chauncey was staying with Jack even though I was home. I wasn't well and Wendy, who was visiting family in Winnipeg, thought that best. It was "pool" day and Jack arrived with Chauncey who, though excited to see me, happily carried on with Jack when he was finished. About an hour after they left, I received a phone call from Jack who was calling from his car down at Ambleside beach in West Vancouver. Chauncey and the Dobermans had gone swimming and Chauncey had collapsed. Jack took him down to our vet, near the Seymour River and Marine Drive, who told me that there was little hope. In fact, he said, "I can take him to a specialist but I don't think he'll make it that far." I wanted to go down and be with them but I was no longer allowed to drive and a taxi, if I could get one, was prohibitive. Jack stayed with Chauncey and held him when he was put down. Having done that with Clancy, I knew how terrible an experience that was.

After the deed was done, Jack called me and said he would like to come up and see me. He duly arrived and I had to tell him that there was no beer in the house. I no longer drink hard liquor but I knew that Wendy had some Irish whiskey so, to hell with my being "on the wagon", he and I sat down with a triple whiskey each to soften the blow! We both wept like children. It was a terrible day made all the worse when I had to phone Winnipeg and tell Wendy.

One of my prized possessions is a beautiful painting of Chauncey, head cocked as if he had just been told it was "swim time", by good friend Rod Gildersleeve. I look at it a lot. So does Wendy.

CHAUNCEY THE TALKING DOG

If you think dogs can't count, try putting three dog biscuits in your pocket and then give him only two of them.
– Phil Pastoret
(author of Our Boarding House, my favourite comic strip)

July 2011:

I've been a bachelor this past week as Wendy has been in Winnipeg visiting her daughter and young granddaughter. When Madeleine was born a year ago, Wendy made it clear that she wasn't going to be like I was—an absentee grandparent (six of my eight grew up in Toronto or Kamloops) and I heartily supported that decision. She takes off a week every other month to visit Maddy and that's great with me—except that leaves me alone with Chauncey, our chocolate Labrador Retriever.

Until Wendy went on her first grandmotherly sojourn I

thought that we more or less divided the dog responsibilities equally. Not so. Not so by a long shot I learned, as I performed *her* tasks too.

First thing in the morning as I'm trying to do for me the impossible—make a cup of coffee, pour some cereal into a bowl adding milk, and get some orange juice for my two vitamin pills, Chauncey arrives completely destroying my concentration.

"What do you want, Chauncey?" I ask, trying to disguise my annoyance.

I scratch my head and there's the answer—he gets a certain kind of biscuit called a toothbrush every morning at that time so I break my complicated routine and get him one, then repair to the sunroom table for breakfast and the papers. But there he is, staring at me, head cocked and raised ears.

"What the hell is it now, Chauncey?"

Oh, yes, he must have his collar on. And then I get ten minutes peace, which is fine because it only takes about seven minutes to read the Vancouver papers with most of the time on the comics—it takes longer to read the *Globe and Mail's* BC section.

Then it starts. He hits me using his tilted head, raised ears pose. I know what this means—his swim. The most important time of his day, by far. But because of my knees I can't take him down the considerable hill to the beach and back so we've hired a neighbour, Trudi, whom Chauncey loves, as surrogate beach goer. But she's not due for an hour so how to amuse him so he doesn't use his final, fatal weapon and start barking? I play with him and seem to be getting away with it when the phone rings, at which time Chauncey starts to bark.

Damn! I forgot it's Monday and CBC Political Panel time, which, ironically, I'm not doing in studio so I can look after Chauncey. I beat a hasty retreat to the loo and do the bit sitting on the john with muffled yet still pretty loud barks coming through the closed door.

As it ends, Trudi arrives, the barks become painful puppy squeaks (he's nearly nine years old), and I have an hour to myself, which I use downstairs in my office eliminating the emails that seem to take quite an interest in the size of my penis and what I can make it do, with their help.

On the dot, Chauncey's back, grinning from ear to ear and sopping wet. There is no expression of joy to match the grin of a sopping wet Labrador Retriever! This means time for what he knows as scrub-a-dub-dub, the vigorous towelling down—with as much effort as possible to the ears, please! I must admit, we both have fun! Finally I'm done—with me as wet as he is now dry—whereupon it's time to fill his water and food dishes and I can finally get back to the computer and the writing tasks for the day.

Except, I hardly get started when Chauncey comes running down stairs, his sort of wool duck, called, ingeniously, "Duck", in his mouth and raising hell. Of course, it's the right day and right time for Jack, the hot tub maintenance man, whom Chauncey adores and the feeling is mutual. If Jack had half a dozen Chaunceys on his route, he'd never be done, as playtime is at least ten, maybe fifteen minutes. Duck is thrown, Chauncey catches and retrieves. Duck is thrown over the fence into the woods next door, Chauncey chases and returns it along with a tennis ball he's found. If you ever wonder why they call them retrievers, drop around our place some time.

Farewell to Jack and now to that article my partner Damien Gillis wants for the website as soon as possible. Deep into my writing mode I go and the words are flying onto the screen—sort of, given my hunt and peck typing style—and damned if Chauncey isn't back! What bloody well now?

Of course! It's 11:00 a.m. and it's "go across the street and be a good boy" time.

Off we go and just inside the gate of the dog path we meet an enormous dog, sort of like a Great Dane but not. Chauncey is a lover, not a fighter, so when he disappears behind a bush chasing the tennis ball I've just thrown, and this other dog attacks him, his mistress starts screaming blue murder, I wonder what could have happened. I apologize—even though Chauncey wants no part of the scrap—and as we get the dogs apart, the other dog starts to hump Chauncey using a very firm grip. We finally separate them and the lady says, accusingly, "Isn't your dog neutered?" to which I say, "No, but for God's sake, he's not gay!"

That done with, we cross the road to our townhouse and I think this is a good time to go through the compound to the store and get the mail.

"Come on, Chauncey, but please don't ..." at which time, even though he's just been across the road "to be a good boy" he dumps right on the compound driveway area and I've used the last of my doggy bags. Besides which, bending down with my knees is a major undertaking. I'm rescued by a neighbour who, with understandable reluctance, does my work for me.

Get the mail, Chauncey with tennis ball firmly in the iron jaws, back home, take off his leash, get the ball, and put it away, and shit! He's bugging me again!

Right, I forgot you get a treat, a bone marrow, when you drop the tennis ball. How stupid of me!

Finally, it's lunchtime so I make myself a toasted, very old cheddar sandwich. And there's Chauncey, in his cocked head staring mode, right beside me.

"What the hell is it now?" We don't feed him at the table but then I remember. When Wendy makes this for me she always puts a bit of cheese in his bowl. Right.

Back to the computer and on the adjacent couch Chauncey settles in for a nice long snooze. I finally get back to work.

But I know what's next.

At 2:58 p.m. Chauncey stirs, stretches, and yawns for a bit. Slowly, at 2:59 p.m. he rises and at 3:00 p.m. precisely, there he is in his "let's get with it" look. Time for his afternoon walk; so it's back over to the doggie path and the usual stuff, including tossing a stick. As any Lab lover knows, a stick trumps a tennis ball any time.

Back home, I know all will be well until I go out for supper, except—what's that bloody dog whining about upstairs? His food and water, I'd forgotten, and with Chauncey, those things do not go unnoticed.

Back to the computer and I put my head down just for a moment, and half an hour later I wake up. Damn! It's time for the dreaded treadmill, then out for dinner at the Olive and Anchor in Horseshoe Bay and a plate of delicious Saltspring mussels and a brew, maybe two. (To cops who may read this, I go down and back on the Toonerville trolley, as we affectionately call our rickety bus, which, in fact, provides excellent service and has wonderful drivers.)

Sufficiently victualed, I arrive home ten minutes late and from the moment I step off the bus I hear Chauncey—I'm 100 yards away and he's inside the townhouse and I can hear him as, no doubt, can most of the neighbourhood. You aren't allowed to be late with Chauncey and it's no excuse that the bus got behind. I open the door and he's barking as only he can bark because it's time for me—indeed ten minutes behind time—to get a ball and go on the deck for twelve, precisely, throws.

That done, his water dish filled, yet another brew for me—I'm feeling pretty smoothened by this time—back to the computer and the blog for Damien is done and, the saints be praised, it's the nightcap hour where I finally get to read a bit and sip yet another brew ... bloody hell, here's that dog in that position again!

It's cookie time—one of those huge ones that cost $1.75 each. As I said to the pet store guy, "Rene, buying the expensive, highly pedigreed dog is the cheap part!" Then, having barely finished his cookie, there he is again with that stupid duck in his mouth. How could I forget—this is the time Wendy throws that damned thing out into the kitchen for him to once again show off his retrieving skills. You must start and once started, you dare not stop.

Finally, it's ten o'clock, time to go "across the road and be a good dog" again, then to bed, and a bit of a read and sleep.

I don't even open the book; I'm out of it the moment my head hits the pillow. I can't understand why.

Honey ... come home!!!

WHEN WE WERE BAD ...

All children should be beaten, though not necessarily as a punishment. The benefits can be extended to the goody-goodies by using beating as a ritual acceptance of authority. Unlike (say) Rugby Union or skiing it raises no health and safety issues.
– Lincoln Allison, Emeritus Reader in Politics at the University of Warwick and Visiting Professor of Sport and Leisure at the University of Brighton (2010!)

Corporal punishment was widely used both at home and at school when serious discipline was required. In public schools the implement used was "the strap" on the palm of the hand. St George's School, which I attended 1942-1946, was modelled after an English Public School like the headmaster's alma mater, Rugby. Corporal punishment was exclusively used and not only could the Masters beat you, so could prefects, older boys given disciplinary powers.

Punishment was caning by a thin and supple strip of bamboo

across the ass, the number of strokes depending upon the offence. The standard garden-variety was three strokes, which jumped to six for smoking and more serious offences; for very serious offences it was eight. Three wasn't too bad but six or eight was a pretty nasty hiding.

The procedure was that you went into the Masters office or the prefects' Common Room, bent over a chair, and took your medicine. It hurt like hell although few would dare admit it. One charming habit of prefects was to sit in the back row of Chapel in the morning and, as we young lads came in, note who had their shoes well shined, and those who didn't were told to "see me afterwards", meaning three of the best. Somehow this didn't seem appropriate for a chapel.

Many of my classmates accepted this crap as "being a man", the stuff English-type schools peddled. One day in 1945 after a fellow named Parker, our home master, came into the classroom and noted that it was boisterous and noisy, as thirteen-year-old boys might well be, he sentenced us all to four hours of detention on Saturday morning. He offered us the alternative of "six of the best". Young boys, being what they are, shamed each other into taking the beating, which nearly everyone took. Those who didn't were chickenshit and mocked mercilessly.

Parker was an enthusiastic beater. It was a hell of a price to pay for being a noisy kid when the teacher was out of the room, and part of the brutality that prevailed.

A few years ago, I met my childhood pal, Denis Hargrave, for the first time in probably sixty years. Over a Scotch, I asked him what he remembered most about St George's. Tears came to his eyes and he said, "The public flogging—as if it were yesterday."

So did I—it had never left me. Here's what happened.

We were youngsters in Grade VII. Five seniors were caught with a stolen car and the magistrate committed them to the Headmaster's "care" on his undertaking to administer suitable punishment. The boys undoubtedly came to wish that the magistrate had just done his duty.

The entire school from Grade VII up was summoned to assembly, where the headmaster told the story. All five miscreants were lined up against the front wall and the gymnasium horse was brought out. One by one, they bent over the horse and were administered the appointed punishment. The ringleader received fifteen strokes, two others got twelve, one got ten, and the last one got eight. The masters who administered the punishments did so with considerable vigour, if not pleasure, and occasionally got tired and turned the cane over to a colleague! One or two canes broke. All but the first guy, who despite getting a brutal fifteen never made a sound, screamed.

For kids our age, it was horrible to witness, made all the more hideous by the last lad, the one to get eight, who fainted. The masters tried to drag him up, drape him over the horse and hold him down but it wasn't possible because he struggled so much. He was remanded until after the Christmas holidays, about two months later, when he would "take his medicine". In due course the date arrived, the assembly was reassembled, and he was brought to the horse kicking and screaming, held down, and given his eight strokes.

A few years ago, I was made "Georgian Of The Year", an honour I would only accept if it were understood that when I came to speak I would relate the story of the flogging. How the current students took it I can't say but it was an obvious relief for older guys who had kept it bottled up for so many years. In its time, however, this brutality was accepted. Mercifully, in the 1970s, beating in the schools was forbidden and it slowly became unacceptable in the home.

I had my own personal moment.

When I was twelve, I visited my Gram and Gandi at their farm in Burnaby (yes, in Burnaby). Outside my bedroom was a bookcase and in it were two silver dollars, one George V, the other George VI, owned by my Aunt Peggy who was "in harm's way" as we now say, driving an ambulance in war-torn Belgium. I stole the coins, went to the local store, bought cigarettes and candy, and shared them with my friend Jack from across the street.

Gram discovered the loss and quizzed me about it. I lied through my teeth. I couldn't admit to her I was a thief! I was to admit much more before long. When I got home my father knew all the facts because the store had reported getting the silver dollars, had described me, and my friend Jack had confessed. Finally, after lying to my dad for quite a while, I confessed too.

Dad beat me within an inch of my life with a plank. This was no spanking. I was black and blue from the small of my back to behind the calves of my legs, no doubt at least partly due to my struggling. My relationship with Dad was never quite the same again.

I'd been very wrong and certainly deserved serious punishment—but not this. That, however, was how kids were punished then and I attach no blame to my father for doing what everyone else did. It was just wrong and I'm glad the times have changed. I loved Dad very much and owe him a huge debt—but that beating was like an elephant in the room for us from then on. In later years we nearly spoke of it from time to time but never could quite make it. I wonder how many other father-son relationships of those days were similarly affected.

In the result, I never laid a finger on any of my four children nor would I send my son to a private school.

MY OH MY IT WAS DIFFERENT …

My grandfather once told me that there were two kinds of people: those who do the work and those who take the credit. He told me to try to be in the first group; there was much less competition.
– Indira Gandhi

Staying with my Gandi and Gram was great fun. Gandi spent time teaching me about the outdoors. He showed me moss on the north side of trees and told me about fireweed, which only grew where there had been a fire. Gandi couldn't tell me where the fireweed was before the fire. I have long puzzled about such phenomena. Across the street from our home, for example, was a vacant lot where an excavation was dug but abandoned and within a couple of days was full of water and frogs. Where the hell did the frogs come from?

Gandi had a miserable and pugnacious Bantam rooster named

Jiggs who used to attack me anytime I came near. As a seven year old I was scared stiff of him. One day Gandi cut off a perfect piece of maple and made me a slingshot and, at the first opportunity, I got Jiggs right in the ass with a piece of cinder from the pathway. He never bothered me again! Gandi was very proud and, more importantly, so was Gram when we told her.

Gandi taught me some great life lessons; such as, it was best to strangle a chicken because cutting its head off was so messy. I can't tell you how often that information was useful for me in later life!

There was a farm worker, or "Chinaman" as we called them back then, whose name was Lee Yuen. He lived in a small house on the farm and he used to give me enormous Chinese oranges. Where he got them in the middle of a war I have no idea. Lee used to smoke a huge water pipe, an exercise that fascinated me, and I have often wondered just what it was he smoked!

Gandi would take me with his German Shepherd, Colonel, and his Springer Spaniel, Tippy, to Still Creek where he taught Tippy to retrieve. Gandi was a devoted duck hunter and fisherman; I inherited just the fishing part. Still Creek is still there and I'm told it holds a small run of Coho thanks to a local fishing club. If so, bless 'em. Gandi instilled in me a love and fascination for the out-of-doors that never left. All kids should have a Gandi and a place to learn.

Denis Hargrave and I used to ride our bikes from our place down Marine Drive to the Musqueam Indian Reservation about two miles away where we would fish in what we knew as Tin Can Creek. There were lots of little fish that I now know were cutthroat trout. We used a tiny hook and a bit of worm and if we caught a few we would clean and try to eat them. They weren't much of a meal!

Interestingly, we were always made welcome.

One day a First Nations lad, perhaps fifteen, came along with a gaff in his hand. He walked slowly up the side of this small creek, went down on his hands and knees, and a few moments later thrust the gaff into the water and pulled out a very substantial Coho Salmon, perhaps five or six pounds! We were aghast! If we had thought that fish that size were there we would've been too scared to fish it. The lad went upstream a ways, did the same thing, and then gave me one of them, which I took home. So unbelievable was my story, Dad was certain I'd stolen the fish and threatened to give me a licking if I didn't tell the truth!

I learned a lifetime lesson from this—Coho salmon spawn in the damnedest places. Most people think that they spawn in huge numbers in large rivers as Pink or Sockeye do but in fact they use tiny creeks, just a few fish per stream, which is why they're in such trouble in populated areas. Developers, hearing that there are only a few fish in a creek, allege that there are no "appreciable fish values" thus they can develop freely. Municipal councils, wanting the revenue, agree and stream by stream we've lost our Coho Salmon. Now we know all about the Coho and its spawning habits, but in many areas it's too late.

Farmers have long resisted any obligation to concern themselves with spawning Coho in their streams and ditches, holding that farms and their produce trump all other concerns. Tin Can Creek, properly called Musqueam Creek, on the other hand, has been carefully preserved by the Band and has one of the very few Coho runs left in the Lower Mainland. As this is being written, the Vancouver Parks Board is rehabilitating New Brighton Park, including a trout stream. Would that we did more of this and fewer pipelines and dams.

Denis and I consider ourselves to be the first nude swimmers at Wreck Beach on the Fraser River, near the Simon Fraser Memorial. The beach is now a famous nude beach but in those days nobody swam there. We would have a swim without the nuisance of a bathing suit even though swimming was and still is considered dangerous in the tricky river current.

One day we swam out to an old hulk, found a large anchor, and managed to get it to shore. This was a Kedge-style anchor, probably the most ancient style of all—the same type as Popeye has tattooed on his forearm. Somehow, with the anchor straddling both bicycles, we managed to walk it home to my place, an enormous effort for a couple of eleven year olds, and when we got there, we were exhausted. We dumped it on my front lawn just as my Dad arrived home from work.

He looked at the anchor, then us, then the anchor again, and asked, "What the Sam hell do you intend doing with that?"

That question had never occurred to us! What the devil *were* we going to do with it? Dad made it abundantly clear that it wasn't staying on the front lawn nor going to the back lawn either. The anchor wound up in a vacant lot right next door and I've often wondered what happened when the lot was developed and the contractors found it. Did they phone the nearest historical society and suggest that it probably belonged to Simon Fraser or some other explorer? Perhaps Sir Francis Drake who, in spite of bleating from San Franciscans, did come this far north? How else could an anchor have found its way to a vacant lot at 6391 McCleery?

Denis and I found another spot and I rather wonder whether it's still there. We would take our bikes along SW Marine Dr past all of the ritzy houses including that of the Reifels (who earned their money, ahem, exporting liquor to the US during Prohibition) to where the road curves up toward Marpole. In there was a swamp, I don't know how big because we were just young kids and it sure as hell looked big to us!

It was so out of character that it was particularly exciting. It was as you would expect a swamp like Okefenokee in the US South to look, a lake out of which grew gloomy trees and on the tree branches were long tresses of pale green moss. The swamp was full of newts, salamanders, and other crawly things that we had never seen before. All in all it was pretty scary but we were drawn back to it time and time again.

Just a few years ago, I was in an art shop in Terrace, BC, and discovered a painting by a BC artist, Anita Desnoyers, which was a perfect reflection of our swamp. I bought the painting and it has pride of place in our living room. I find I can't look at it without getting shivery but still longing in a way to go back and see it again, in the flesh, so to speak.

I must conclude with a note about the Simon Fraser Memorial. It was known to us kids when teens as "Strugglers Gulch", the place we went to neck after the movie. To say that it was very popular would be a gross understatement. The reason we had to drive so far was that the Vancouver cops pestered hell out of you everywhere else and this was RCMP territory. Presumably they had once been teenagers themselves. Interestingly, I don't ever remember a girl saying, "Oh no, don't take me out to the Gulch, take me home to mother."

VANCOUVER YESTERDAY AND TODAY

Tempora mutantur et nos mutamur in illis. "The times change, and we change with them."

– John Lyly

Of course Vancouver has changed a great deal since I was a boy. It has grown from a town of about 300,000 people to over two-million in the greater Vancouver area. There has been an enormous influx of newcomers, many from China and Taiwan, many from India, and many from all parts of the globe. This has meant adjustments, not all of them easy to make but all of which are being made. A huge plus is, of course, in the restaurants, which represent virtually every nation in the world. One of the nice things about these eateries is that many are located in various neighbourhoods so that you can be in a residential area and find, close by, a first-class ethnic restaurant.

The neighbourhoods themselves have really not changed very much, with the exception of the West End, which has gone from basically single dwellings to large apartment houses. There still is a well-defined Chinatown, there is a district that has a large Italian population as it always did, and so on. When I occasionally revisit the 6300-6400 block McCleery, there are the chestnut trees I knew, there are the two houses I lived in, and there's the old neighbourhood sans Baroness Van Steenwyck's Dairy Farm and sans our marvellous woods. The road patterns have stayed pretty well as they always have been and I daresay that if my grandfathers were to come back today they would say it has sure grown a lot but it still looks like it always did.

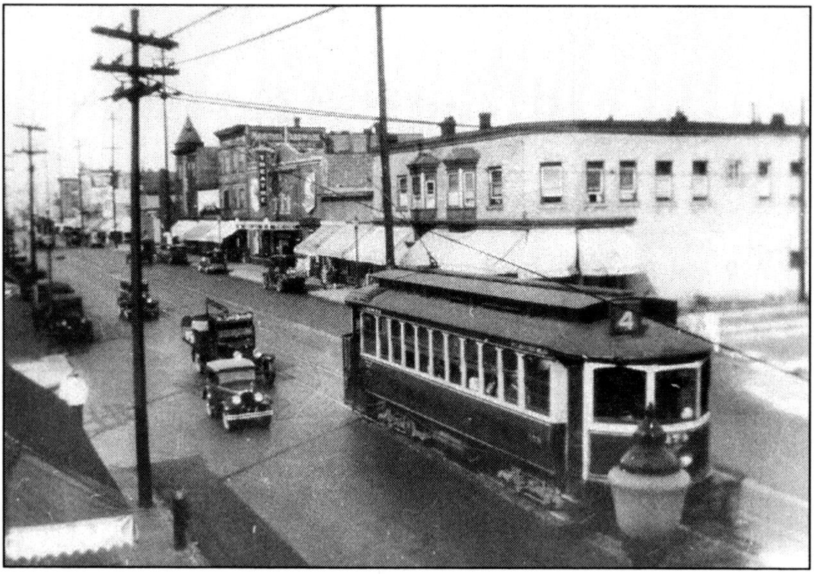

Commercial drive in the 30s.

Little Italy when that's what it was.

Photo courtesy of the City of Vancouver Archives

Because of the changes in demographics, Vancouver is a much more cosmopolitan city than ever. This permits me a bit of an editorial comment. I suppose everyone would like to have that nice old hometown they grew up in. In fact, I can say, not me. I loved Vancouver as it was and no one could be luckier than I was to have grown up here. However, Vancouver is a much better place now than it was. We have learned to be tolerant, which is not to say we all love one another—a state of affairs that would probably be too tiresome to accept anyway! We have a modern city but have been able to retain the charm that the beauty around us demands.

We remain in a glorious setting with a climate pretty easy to take. I always laugh at visitors who complain about the rain. I tell them that the explanation my mother gave me when I was a little boy wanting the rain to go away was that without the rain we wouldn't have the tall trees and the green grass and all of the nice surroundings. Evidently my response was, "Couldn't God give us less rain and smaller trees?"

If it's raining in Vancouver and you see someone with a hat, an overcoat, an umbrella, and possibly galoshes, then you know that person is from Edmonton or Toronto or Halifax. If you see a man with his jacket collar pulled up over his ears and holding a newspaper over his head you know he's from Vancouver. We are in denial. Vancouverites have a pretty blasé view of rain. It can pour for a week but when the sun comes out and glistens off the water and the mountains, that week of rain is completely forgotten and the question is "what rain?"

As I write this it's the 18th of February and it's 18 degrees below zero Celsius in Toronto. Wendy just returned from visiting her family in Winnipeg where it was 40 below with the wind chill factor. Eastern Canada is expecting an ice storm from Siberia, according to the CBC. The rest of the country is also freezing and covered in snow. In Vancouver it's 14 degrees Celsius, about 58 Fahrenheit. The Japanese Cherries are in full bloom, the daffodils are out, and lawns are being mowed. As the old saying has it, the thing about rain is you don't have to shovel it. I rest my case!

Of course, for reasons I cannot explain, British Columbia is not for everyone. Thank God for that—we have quite enough people. My advice to those from other parts of Canada who are thinking of moving to Vancouver is to come here in November and if you still want to be here by March 1 you'll make it. Better still, stay put and bask in your self-imposed superiority and forget all about the weather.

YOU'VE GOTTA TALK SALMON

Cynic—a man who knows the price of everything and the value of nothing.
– Oscar Wilde

One of the things the world thinks of when British Columbia is mentioned—probably the first thing—is the salmon, which, in all its forms has been an immense benefit, part of our soul ... and, for Ottawa, a perpetual political pain in the ass. As you will see, defining the salmon is complicated and the competition for it intense.

I'm going to deal with the value of the west coast fishery but not in terms of money because money is all but irrelevant. My comments are around the words of Dr. Brian Riddell, a fish scientist who left the Department of Fisheries accusing the Federal bureaucracy of not acting on advice from those who knew their business. He remarked that, in his opinion, "Ottawa is abandoning wild Pacific salmon because they don't see their value."

If this was just a throwaway line from a disgruntled former government employee it could be ignored but Dr. Riddell isn't that sort. He has an impeccable record as a scientist and a man who calls it as he sees it. Moreover, the charge rings true based on much evidence that his allegation is accurate going back decades. To put it in its simplest form—the Pacific Salmon has been a political pain in the ass for Ottawa since 1871, the time of Confederation.

First, let's get the technicalities down. There are nine separate species of Pacific salmon but only seven of them apply to us, as two are Asian. Dealing with the salmonids is difficult for laypersons because often their common name is incorrect, starting with the Pacific Salmon.

The two fish *properly* called "salmon" are the Atlantic Salmon (*Salmo Salar*) and the Brown Trout (*Salmo Trutta*), neither of which is native to the West Coast although Brown Trout have been planted in some local rivers including the Cowichan on Vancouver Island.

Let's let the dead language, Latin, do the work for us as we identify what we have on the West Coast. What we've traditionally but wrongly called "salmon" is the Oncorhynchus family including Chinook, Chum, Coho, Sockeye, and Pink. Until about twenty years or so ago, two other salmonids, the Rainbow Trout (Steelhead if they migrate into the Ocean) and Cutthroat Trout, were thought to be true trout (*Salmo*) but those who know about these things re-designated them as Pacific Salmon

(Oncorhynchus) some twenty-five years ago. Hence seven species in BC, five of which are fished commercially.

The Chars (*Salvelinus*)—confusingly called trout though they're not—include Bull Trout, Lake Trout, Brook Trout (not native but imported into several lakes and streams), and Dolly Varden Trout (perhaps just a variety of Bull Trout). They needn't concern us in this discussion as they are mostly sports fish found in fresh water but they are a big issue as threatened species in the private energy program of the Campbell-Clark government.

For many years, the argument raged as to whether sports fishing or commercial fishing was more valuable and it is this that creates a false dichotomy, an argument that trivializes both. If you start to put a value on Pacific salmon, you're essentially evaluating the value of water products of all sorts and that brings in a new player—hydroelectric power. And here come the damn dams.

Hydroelectric power is anathema to migrating fish as the Grand Coulee Dam on the Columbia long ago demonstrated. A dam blocks access to the spawning grounds of returning salmon. It's possible to use ladders to get some returning fish above the dam but no satisfactory way of getting the fry downstream has yet been discovered. The dam literally castrates the spawning salmon. We learned that lesson from the Grand Coulee Dam in Washington.

Construction of Grand Coulee Dam began in 1933, was completed in 1942, and is the largest hydropower producer in the United States with a total generating capacity of 6,809 megawatts. The W.A.C. Bennett and Revelstoke Dams together have a capacity of about 5,500 megawatts, while BC Hydro's thirty integrated hydroelectric generating stations, two gas-fired thermal power plants, and one combustion turbine station, have a total installed generating capacity of about 11,000.

In 1948, there was a huge flood on the Fraser River (as a high schooler I helped do the sandbagging), and flood control was a hot topic. It was said—especially by dam builders—that a dam was required on the Fraser River. What would a dam on the Fraser be like?

In 1952, American financiers proposed building the biggest dam in the world, at that time, at Moran Canyon north of Lytton on the Fraser River. The plan called for a 270-metre-high dam, backing the Fraser up into a 260-kilometre lake, stretching upstream to Quesnel. The developers and their supporters maintained that the dam would hold back silt, allowing the Fraser to be navigable by deep-sea vessels to Chilliwack, and flooding would no longer be a risk in the Lower Mainland. It was said that the dam, being north of Lytton, wouldn't impede spawning salmon that turn right at Lytton and go up the Thompson to the Adams River. I haven't, however, seen any studies as to what would happen to water levels below the dam and if that could be a problem for the Adams River Run and other species. What it *would* do is exterminate the Sockeye, which go north at Lytton, a very significant loss, especially to First Nations.

The deal looked like this—hydroelectric capacity would be equal to the Grand Coulee and two Hoover dams combined. An aluminum smelter and uranium processing plant were part of the equation. God only knows what the hydro electric capacity would be if other dams were later involved. And here's where the concrete and the fish collide; for promoters to make this happen politically, they know that the northern sockeye would have to disappear and thus no longer be an issue. If the major sockeye run that goes through the Thompson at Lytton into the Fraser were to fail, that would open up even more opportunities for hydro-power, and who could now protest? The political key to shutting up environmentalist nuisances is the absence of migratory fish to protect. Imagine the profits involved in this sort of Hydro development! The Moran Dam project is dusted off occasionally and certainly exists in the minds of those who slaver at the thought of huge hydro projects.

The Atlantic salmon fish farm is a story in itself. There is no doubt that disease and sea lice from these fish destroy wild salmon smolts. Science keeps telling us this, and the redoubtable Alexandra Morton keeps fighting her valiant fight, but the governments do nothing.

It's for these reasons we must understand that those who would save the fish can't possibly win the "money" fight. This is like the agricultural land debate, which, if dealt with on the basis of the monetary value of the land alone, would soon have all farmland paved and developed. If we have decided as a society that money is not the issue with protecting farmland, it shouldn't be with salmon either. The debate should include values—social values and moral values. The salmon is a symbol known around the world as British Columbia. More importantly for First Nations, it is the symbol of their cultures as well as the food they rely upon. Of course, it also employs a lot of people. It's just plain wrong to exterminate our fish for any reason whatsoever and we must force developers, fish farmers, and governments to come into our ring to fight; a ring where values are more important than money.

Stick to the salmon and we can win—talk about monetary issues and we lose. It's as simple as that.

ONE SUNDAY MORNING … BOOM!

No bastard ever won a war by dying for his country. He won it by making the other poor dumb bastard die for his country.

– George S. Patton

The world suddenly changed one day.

On Sunday morning, 3 September 1939, I was sitting up a chestnut tree near our house when a newsboy came down the street hollering, "Extra, extra, war declared—read all about it!" World War II had arrived.

My parents had spoken about a coming war for some time and although I was scared, I wasn't quite sure what I was scared about. One day Mom talked about hiring a German maid and my Auntie Lo said, "I hope she isn't a 'Nancy'", and I couldn't figure out why her name mattered. I was soon to learn all about "Nazis".

That afternoon, the neighbourhood men talked about events

and though the war was only a few hours old, there were rumours galore. It was said that a large German warship had been sunk. In fact, there *was* a ship sunk—the UK luxury liner, the *Athenia*, by a German U-boat off the coast of Ireland with 128 dead. The Nazi Propaganda Minister, Josef Goebbels, insisted it was sunk by the Royal Navy but it wasn't.

I remember several things about April 1940 and the end of the "Phoney War". My parents and all grown-ups showed great strain as Hitler swallowed up Denmark, occupied Norway, and invaded France and the Lowlands. France fell and I well remember Mr. Hargrave, my pal Denis's dad, driving us to school in his old Ford Model "T" and telling us about Dunkirk and the miraculous evacuation of the British Expeditionary Force; I remember Gracie Fields and her "There'll Always be an England"; I recall my Dad and me listening to (probably) a re-broadcast of Churchill's "Finest Hour" speech and the tears running down my Dad's face. We listened to all Churchill's speeches and later to Roosevelt's "fireside chats".

We didn't suffer during the war. Actually, we were bloody lucky for when kids came out from England to our school, we learned about the Blitz and what it was like to be sent so far away, leaving your parents behind. Many of these boys boarded at the school all year with only letters from home for occasional comfort. We then had an idea of how others suffered.

We certainly knew and understood nothing about the suffering of Japanese Canadian kids who in early 1942 suddenly disappeared from sight to wind up in internment camps. As a child I was firmly reprimanded by my parents for asking the obvious and embarrassing question about the statue in Stanley Park dedicated to Japanese Canadians who fought and died fighting for Canada in World War I.

There was some rationing, meaning that we couldn't get as much sugar as usual and that my dad had to borrow non-drinkers' liquor licenses to keep up the domestic supply! Gas was rationed, leading to the new crime of siphoning somebody else's tank.

The big worry for us came when Uncle Howard Bardon joined the Duke of Connaught's Own Rifles (DCORs) and was quickly dispatched overseas. Uncle Howard was the perfect English officer, tall and thin, with a brisk moustache looking as if he'd been born with a swagger stick under his arm. Being English, he couldn't wait to join up and was one of the first to go overseas to Britain.

A later friend of mine, the late Bob White, was with the Seaforth Highlanders and was on a troop ship from Africa to Italy with Uncle Howard's outfit when it was torpedoed. He told me, "We were all mustered on deck but no one could find Bardon. In due course he appeared in full dress uniform and announced that 'if he was going down, it would be as a British soldier and a gentleman!' The ship, in the event, stayed afloat." That was Uncle Howard, all right.

I remember 1941 and listening, with my Dad, to Churchill's famous speech directed to America dealing with the state of Britain at that time and closing with this famous bit:

"The other day President Roosevelt gave his opponent in the late Presidential election a letter of introduction to me, and in it he wrote out a verse in his own handwriting, from Longfellow, which, he said, "applies to you people as it does to us." Here is the verse:

Sail on, O Ship of State!
Sail on, O Union, strong and great!
Humanity with all its fears
With all the hopes of future years
Is hanging breathless on thy fate!

What is the answer that I shall give in your name to this great man, the thrice-chosen head of a nation of 130,000,000? Here is the answer which I will give to President Roosevelt.

Put your confidence in us. Give us your faith and your blessing, and under Providence all will be well. We shall not fail or falter; we shall not weaken or tire. Neither the sudden shock of battle nor the long-drawn trials of vigilance and exertion will wear us down. Give us the tools and we will finish the job."

For Canadians, there was the famous visit of Churchill to our Parliament on 30 December 1941, a speech memorable for two things. Churchill had his portrait done by Karsh in the Speaker's chambers (where the spot is duly recorded with a plaque). The story has it that Karsh, under the cloth cover used in those days for portrait photography, reached out and grabbed Churchill's cigar from his hand whereupon Churchill flashed anger, which was how the famous portrait of Churchill scowling became famous throughout the world.

His speech was memorable indeed. Having traced the course of the war to the fall of France, Churchill said, "*When I warned them* [the French] *that Britain would fight on alone whatever they did their generals told their Prime Minister and his divided Cabinet, 'In three weeks England would have her neck wrung like a chicken.' Some chicken! Some Neck.*"

It was heady stuff and any who doubt the pivotal role Churchill played in keeping Britain going obviously didn't hear Churchill speak during those dark days. I became a life-long hero worshipper and I'm now considered a Churchillian and am often asked to speak on the great man.

As I say, I was a precocious kid! We had a short wave band on our radio and I found the station from the USSR that carried the news in English. In 1942, my Dad hung up a huge map in my bedroom along with little flagged pins so I could plot the movement of the various armies in the field. My friend Dave Rolfe and I spent hours poring over news and keeping track of where everybody was. We stuck pins with flags on my big map to show where armies were at any particular time. I especially remember the Soviet pins moving back and forth until the Battle of Stalingrad in November of 1942 and the great tank battle at Kursk in May–June 1943. After that, the flags mostly went from right to left on my map.

Dave and I each, at different times, won the General Knowledge prize at St George's, beating out all the seniors. Why I don't know, but I remember the key question in one test being "Who was the captain of the *H.M.S. Jervis Bay* who posthumously received the Victoria Cross?" I had the only correct answer in the school—"Fogarty Fegan" (as Casey Stengel used to say, "You could look it up").

On Sunday, 7 December 1941, I was over at Denny's place when Mr. Hargrave came out and informed us that Japan had bombed Pearl Harbour in the Hawaiian Islands. The next day we heard President Roosevelt open his speech to a joint hearing of Congress thusly:

> *"Yesterday, December 7th, 1941—a date which will live in infamy—the United States of America was suddenly and deliberately attacked by naval and air forces of the Empire of Japan.*
>
> The President closed: *"With confidence in our armed forces, with the unbounding determination of our people, we will gain the inevitable triumph—so help us God.*
>
> *"I ask that the Congress declare that since the unprovoked and dastardly attack by Japan on Sunday, December 7th, 1941, a state of war has existed between the United States and the Japanese empire."*

Now Churchill finally had the ally he had prayed for.

My great ambition was to join the Navy. Just why I was so set on this I don't know but I couldn't wait to be old enough to join the Royal Canadian Sea Cadets, which I did in 1944. All of us at St George's were already members of the Royal Canadian Army Cadets and Mom was horrified that her son was learning to bayonet people by practicing on big sacks of straw in two places!

At the top of McCleery Street was a working dairy farm

owned by a Dutch noblewoman, Baroness Van Steenwyck. One day, Dutch Princess Juliana, later Queen, who was living in Ottawa for the duration, came to visit the baroness. As she drove down W47th Ave, all of us kids stood waving Dutch flags. Where we got them from I have no idea! The Princess stopped and said a few words to us and we were thrilled.

Denis lived at the west edge of the large woods between our houses and we became great pals, with the woods our glorious playground. Being wartime, and with us so patriotic, we formed an army called the Red, White, and Blue Gang. Our perpetual foes were the Black Tigers, with the battles mostly consisting of destroying the other guy's fort when he wasn't around.

I was wounded in one of the struggles, not against the Black Tigers but another gang whose name I can't remember. A young "enemy" named Bill Ritchie tossed a fire log over the top of a fence when I happened to be bravely standing guard on the other side. It struck my forehead. Suddenly, all my courage vanished and I ran home through the woods screaming, blood pouring from my head. I was taken to emergency and had several stitches. I have the scar to this day. As it turned out, Bill and I became good friends and ended up fraternity brothers at UBC.

I was bitterly disappointed when the war ended because I'd been trained to be a soldier and a sailor and wanted in very badly; however, five years later a war started in Korea but by that time I had learned a hell of lot, including that you could get killed in war! Some of my friends joined up but I passed.

Without any question, the searing memory of World War II

for me was one day in August 1944 when I was standing on the wharf with Hugh at North Woodlands waiting for the Scenic to bring Nan Nan for a visit at Hatfield's island where I was staying. She got off the boat, went straight to Hugh, also her grandson, and said, "Hugh, your dad has been killed." Looking back, perhaps there was no other way it could have been done, but the shock was horrific.

Hugh loved his dad very much and was enormously proud of him. Uncle Howard was a captain and about to be brevetted a major. He was killed in Italy, near Assisi, when his jeep ran over a land mine and he died a few days later. I had corresponded with Uncle Howard and one time he sent me a shoulder patch from the famous British Eighth Army of then General, later Field Marshall, Viscount Bernard Montgomery of Alamein, the so-called Desert Rats, to which he was attached. I had it sewn on my blazer and I wore it as proudly as if I had been fighting the Afrika Korps myself. His loss was a very sad moment.

Just as the war seemed to be drawing to a successful conclusion, we had a rude awakening. On 6 March 1945, just before noon, when I was at school, there was a tremendous noise and we all jumped up and wondered just what it could be. Had the Japanese finally bombed downtown Vancouver?

It turned out that a 10,000-ton freighter, called the *Greenhill Park,* had exploded, twice in succession. Eight men were killed, nineteen workers were injured, and subsequently a number of firemen and rescue workers were also injured. The explosions called for an extensive investigation under the chairmanship of

Mr. Justice Sidney Smith, which seemed to be inconclusive other than part of the cargo was highly flammable and that somehow it had exploded. A scarcely perspicacious observation.

Much later, one of the crew told quite a different story. According to him, the boys carried a large quantity of alcohol onboard and when one of them went to get a drink and lit a match to help him see, the explosion occurred. The whiskey was 60 percent raw alcohol and highly combustible. Presumably this explosion caused the detonation of the sodium chlorite that formed the major part of the cargo.

In any event, because of the war, the suspicion of sabotage and that sort of thing, this was an international story and great excitement for our city.

WAR TAUGHT KIDS LESSONS OUR PARENTS NEVER LEARNED

We ask for nothing special. We ask only to be permitted to live as you live, and as our nation's Constitution provides.
– Jackie Robinson, the first Afro-American in the Major Leagues in the twentieth century and member of the Hall of Fame

How odd of God
To choose the Jews.
– William Norman Ewer (1885–1976)

But not so odd
As those who choose
A Jewish God
Yet spurn the Jews
– Cecil Brown or Ogden Nash

During the war we heard a great deal about the suffering of Jews in Europe. At home, for over a century, the Vancouver Club—of which I have been a member for nearly fifty years—had a "no Jew" policy. It finally ended in 1977 when the Chief Justice of the BC Supreme Court, Nathan Nemetz, became the first Jewish member—in order to get by the Board of Directors, it took Lieutenant-Governor Walter Owen and Chief Justice John Farris of the Court of Appeal as sponsors. I must admit that I feel ashamed of myself for not having said anything in the eleven years I had by then been a member. It's hard to square our horror about Jews in Europe with our attitude toward them at home.

The Royal Vancouver Yacht Club was the same as the Vancouver Club. My father was a flag officer of the RVYC and one year for the annual party was required to put on a skit. He asked a Jewish chap to write it for him and it was a huge success. When I asked my dad how Hymie enjoyed it, my father said, "Well, of course, he couldn't be there because he's a Jew, you know." Evidently Hymie was good enough to write the script that entertained everybody but not good enough to see his handiwork in action! I withhold severe criticism of my father because that was part and parcel of the way people of his vintage and his social class thought. That doesn't mean that it was okay—far from it—just that it was part of the social mores of the time, just as discrimination against all minorities was.

I'm sure many wondered how our generation would be when we grew up, considering what we were hearing and seeing. Most of the movies we saw were war pictures and after Pearl Harbour they were mostly American showing brave Marines slaughtering slanty-eyed little "Japs" that we all learned to hate. The racial prejudices we learned from those movies and comic books we read were difficult to erase. Similarly, it was hard to look at Germans as human beings after the horrible revelation of the Holocaust. (As an aside, the racial prejudice against the Japanese obscured their great talent at building airplanes and warships—they were supposed to be only capable of cheap imitations of other people's stuff. This foolish prejudice seriously hurt US Intelligence.)

Somehow we survived all this and became different than our parents. In fact, it was our generation, in the '50s, that spawned the revolution of the '60s. We had grown up with the "Four Freedoms" of Churchill and Roosevelt and we believed in them. Jackie Robinson was our post-war big hero as in 1946 he became the first Black to play in organized ball in the twentieth century—in Montreal—and then, in 1947, with the Brooklyn Dodgers, first in the major-leagues.

The event that triggered the massive movement for Black civil rights was the Emmett Till case where a fourteen-year-old black kid from Chicago whistled at a white woman in Money, Miscopy County, in August 1955 and was brutally murdered. The main suspects were acquitted—they always were in Southern states—but later admitted to committing the crime.

Till's mother insisted on a public funeral service, with an open casket to show the world the brutality of the killing: Till had been beaten up and his eye had been gouged out, before he was shot through the head and thrown into the Tallahatchie River with a seventy-pound cotton gin fan tied to his body with barbed wire. His body was in the river for three days before it was discovered and retrieved by two fishermen. Suddenly Southern "society" was under the microscope. There had been no shortage of lynchings but the Till case, because of Till's age and the brutality of the death, hit home with white people everywhere.

In 1962, journalist John Howard Griffin wrote *Black Like Me*. Griffin had his skin died black then set about travelling through the US South as a "black man". This was an eye opener and I well remember not being able to put the book down. The constant humiliations Griffin faced gave a picture of the life of a black in the south, were told in placid but angry tones, and for the first time white people saw life in the south as it really was.

There was another triggering event and many historians date the Civil Rights movement from 1 December 1955 when an unknown black seamstress in Montgomery, Alabama refused to give up her bus seat to a white passenger. This brave woman, Rosa Parks, was arrested and fined for violating a city ordinance, but her lonely act of defiance made her an inspiration to freedom-loving people everywhere. (Incidentally, doing this very thing in 1945 got Lieutenant Jackie Robinson court-martialled—he was acquitted.) Parks' act of defiance triggered the Montgomery Bus Boycott, which resulted in a crippling financial deficit for the Montgomery public transit system because the city's black population, who were the drivers of the boycott, were also the bulk of the system's ridership. The boycott lasted a year and, among other things, gave the great Civil Rights leader Martin Luther King Jr.

and others great and compelling publicity. It broke the back of Segregation.

The freedom fighters in the US South became our heroes. Unless you were alive at the time, you cannot imagine the social changes that took place in a relatively short time and when, in 1964, Lyndon Johnson, a southerner, got the Civil Rights Act passed by Congress, it was a near miracle. Times changed rapidly, too rapidly for some older folks, and a lot of people who really didn't want to change did—but reluctantly.

It took time—far too much time.

In 1963, when I was president of Quilchena Golf Club in Richmond, a gentleman named Lee applied to join and the directors approved him. It wasn't until Mr. Lee came out to the practice fairway that it was discovered he was Chinese. All hell broke loose because Quilchena had a racial ban as an unwritten rule. With Steveston so near, some feared that the club would be swamped by Japanese if "those people" were allowed in.

As president, I decided it was time to put an end to this bullshit and I called a general meeting of the golf club to deal with the issue, once and for all. I was advised not to do this because people would be embarrassed and I would cause dissension. Several of my Board Members were opposed to a meeting but, typically, reluctant to say so publicly. I received many angry phone calls and a couple of nasty threats. I convened the meeting anyway and virtually everybody was there.

Right in front of me at the podium sat an old Scotsman named Bill Campbell, who had spent a terrible war in a Japanese prison camp and it was, naturally, assumed that he was going to raise hell. I gave a speech of which I am, if I may say so, very proud. I then opened up the meeting to questions and the first hand up was Bill Campbell's. Shit! Here it comes! I was ready for the worst.

Bill stood up and in his Scottish brogue said, "Mr. President—when are you going to fill up that damned ditch on the 18th where I'm constantly losing my golf ball?"

There was silence for a moment ... then the whole place started to laugh. The pressure evaporated. I asked if it was time to adjourn to the bar and the yeas were unanimous. It was all over and well past time for it.

Postscript: the Club profited greatly and quickly and has never looked back.

CANADIAN BOMBSHELL: THE FORGOTTEN CASE OF IGOR GOUZENKO

On Sept. 5 he was famously turned away by the RCMP, then … by the night editor of the Ottawa Journal, and finally had to hide his family out across the hall in the neighbour's apartment … until the Ottawa cops turned up.

– David Climenhaga

The story I'm about to relate was of enormous importance and it spawned the Cold War, no less. This story and its impact occupied my teenage years and didn't end until my forties when Richard Nixon resigned. It was hugely embarrassing to Canada, as you will soon see, to the US and the UK. On 5 September 1945, a cipher clerk in the Soviet Embassy named Igor Gouzenko, stationed in Ottawa, learned that he and his family were to be returned to

Moscow. They liked Canada, so he stole 109 secret documents on Soviet espionage but couldn't find anyone to defect to!

Gouzenko went to the RCMP, but the officers on duty refused to believe his story. He then went to the *Ottawa Journal*, but the night editor wasn't interested. He went to the Justice Branch but there was nobody on duty. Knowing that his theft would be discovered and terrified for his family, he hid them in the apartment across the hall for the night as Soviet agents searched his apartment and only left when the police arrived.

Finally, the next day Gouzenko made contact with someone in the RCMP who would listen and who hid him and his family in what became known as "Camp X", outside Ottawa, near Oshawa.

Safely ensconced in Camp X, Gouzenko was interviewed by investigators from Britain's MI5 and from the American FBI but the Keystone Cops fandango wasn't over yet. When the RCMP reported their findings to Prime Minister Mackenzie King he wanted nothing to do with the matter, not wishing to upset our "glorious Russian ally". Even with Gouzenko in hiding under RCMP protection, King wanted to avoid upsetting the Soviet Union. King, then seventy and war weary, was aghast when Norman Robertson, Undersecretary for External Affairs, and his assistant, H. H. Wrong, informed him on September 16 that Gouzenko and his wife Svetlana had gone to Justice Minister Louis St. Laurent with documents unmasking Soviet perfidy on Canadian soil. "It was like a bomb on top of everything else," King wrote.

Robertson told the Prime Minister that Gouzenko was threatening suicide, but King was adamant that his government not get involved, even if Gouzenko was apprehended by Soviet authorities. Robertson ignored the Prime Minister's wishes and authorized asylum to Gouzenko and his family on the basis that their lives were in danger. When word got out in the media (February 1946) that Canadians gave classified information to the Soviet government, it created a great stir.

Canada played an important part in the early nuclear bomb research and was a supplier of uranium—vital information dangerous in the hands of others; thus Gouzenko's defection ushered in the modern era of Canadian security intelligence. Gouzenko's evidence led to the arrest of thirty-nine suspects, of whom eighteen were convicted, including Fred Rose, the only Communist in the Canadian House of Commons, Sam Carr, the Communist Party's national organizer, and scientist Raymond Boyer, found guilty of conspiracy to pass information to the Soviet Union. These three accused pled that their actions were meant to help the anti-Nazi movement but that defence fell on deaf ears. Only half of those arrested and accused were found guilty of lesser charges, which left Canadians with considerable unease.

A Royal Commission, headed by Justices Robert Taschereau and Roy Kellock, was conducted into the Gouzenko Affair, which alerted countries like the US and UK that Soviet agents had almost certainly infiltrated their nations as well.

Gouzenko's testimony was vital in the successful prosecution of Klaus Fuchs, the German communist physicist who had emigrated to Britain, and then gave atomic secrets to Russia. Fuchs worked at the Chalk River Laboratories, near Ottawa, where atomic research had been underway since the early 1940s. His information also likely helped in the investigation and convictions of Julius and Ethel Rosenberg in the US.

Gouzenko is also believed to have assisted with the Venona investigation that eventually led to the discovery of vital Soviet spies such as Donald Maclean, Guy Burgess, Kim Philby, Anthony Blunt, and John Cairncross (the so-called "Cambridge Five"), as well as Alan Nunn May.

The Cold War had started, in Canada, and a lowly cipher clerk named Igor Gouzenko had started it! In the most high profile case arising out of the Gouzenko affair, Julius Rosenberg, thirty-three, and his thirty-five-year-old wife, Ethel, were accused of stealing technical information from the atom research centre in Los Alamos and turning it over to the KGB. A radar expert, Morton Sobell, was also been found guilty of the same charges.

The court heard that the Rosenbergs were involved in a complicated spy ring including Mrs. Rosenberg's brother David Greenglass, former Soviet vice-consul Arkadi Yakovlev, and Philadelphia chemist Harry Gold. Greenglass, a machinist at the Los Alamos research centre during the war, said he had been asked by the Rosenbergs, both committed Communists, to obtain information about the atomic bomb telling the court he was unaware he was working on the atomic bomb project until his brother-in-law, Julius Rosenberg, told him. The information was passed to Harry Gold, who turned it over to the Russians. Gold, who got thirty years after pleading guilty to espionage, worked as a go-between for Klaus Fuchs. Fuchs was jailed for fourteen years in 1950 after admitting that he'd passed atomic secrets to Russia for many years.

The Rosenbergs were sentenced to death and, despite numerous appeals for clemency, were executed by the electric chair at Sing Sing Prison on 19 June 1953, the only people in the United States ever executed for Cold War espionage, and their conviction fuelled US Senator Joseph McCarthy's anti-communist crusade against "anti-American activities" by US citizens. David Greenglass escaped the death penalty, and gained immunity for his wife, after agreeing to give evidence against his sister and brother-in-law. He served ten years in jail. Anatoli Yakovlev, also allegedly involved in the spy ring, escaped trial after fleeing to Russia before the American authorities could catch up with him. And it all started with a lowly clerk in the Soviet Embassy in Ottawa who had a hell of a time getting anyone to listen to him!

The plot thickened.

Part of the spin-off of the Gouzenko saga was the amazing story of Alger Hiss and it, along with the McCarthy witch hunt, was about all that we young University students—as I was back then—interested in politics could talk about. Alger Hiss was a highly respected lawyer and intellectual who, as a US State Department and UN official, helped establish the United Nations. The Hiss case was the centrepiece of many beery debates by members of the UBC Law Class of 1956 down at the Georgia Hotel Pub. For law students interested in fair trials, civil rights, and hearsay evidence this case was almost a year's education in itself!

Here's how it unfolded.

The Hiss saga, which hasn't ended to this day, all started with a strange duck named Whittaker Chambers, once an editor of the conservative *TIME* magazine, who accused Hiss of being a spy. By this time, 1948, the "red scare" was running rampant in America and the House of Representatives set up HUAC (House Committee on Un-American Activities) to deal with this issue.

On 3 August 1948, Chambers, who himself had been a member of the Communist Party, testified to the HUAC that Hiss had secretly been a communist while in federal service. This was interesting because Chambers had previously said that Hiss had never been a communist. Hiss was subpoenaed before the HUAC and emphatically denied that he'd ever been a member of the Communist Party or indeed had done anything disloyal. When Chambers repeated the charge outside the protection of HUAC, Hiss sued for libel.

This ongoing saga saw Hiss go to jail, a mysterious typewriter as a key piece of evidence, incriminating documents allegedly typed by Mrs. Hiss, which probably were forged, all leading to the rise of Richard Nixon, and adding fuel to the vicious lies by Senator Joe McCarthy, whose witch-hunts for Communists nearly tore the nation apart.

Was Hiss guilty?

Probably, but his greatest sin may be the boost his case gave to a young Navy vet named Richard Milhous Nixon, who had won his seat in Congress against Helen Gahagan Douglas, wife of famous actor Melvin Douglas, by implying that she was a communist and a security risk, a vicious lie. At the time the Hiss case broke, Nixon was a first-term Republican Congressman and a member of HUAC. He was a man on the make and in a hurry. It was he who pursued Whittaker Chambers' story when other members of the committee were prepared to drop the matter. Nixon's questionable behaviour in 1948 included colluding with Chambers, leaking secret HUAC testimony, and knowingly offering misleading testimony to the Hiss case grand jury.

Nixon was elected to the US Senate in 1950, was twice elected vice president of the United States (in 1952 and 1956) and was twice elected president (in 1968 and 1972). In 1974, shortly before his expected impeachment by the House of Representatives for his illegal actions that led to the Watergate scandal, he became the first president to resign the office. The Igor Gouzenko case had finally ended.

A hell of a story—a story that started in Canada only to be forgotten by most Canadians, likely because "official" Canada prefer it that way. It has been forgotten by Americans because it is a horrible reminder of their many failings, not least of their denial of civil liberties.

For my generation, it marked our coming of age and sharpened the cynicism that marks the passing of innocence to the discoveries of adulthood.

DÉJÀ VU ALL OVER AGAIN

No one man can terrorize a whole nation unless we are all his accomplices.

– Edward R. Murrow

As this is written in March of 2015, Prime Minister Stephen Harper is playing the age-old game of frightening hell out of the majority by magnifying dangers of a very small minority. Fanatic Islam is threatening the entire world including Canada. There was an attack by such a fanatic on Parliament although there is no evidence that he did so as part of the ISIS Jihad. But it being election time, this is just the moment where an unscrupulous political leader seizes the moment and turns it into an electoral advantage. It's classic George W. Bush, a fellow intellectual of the right, who parlayed the hateful Saddam Hussein and those who looked like him into two election victories from which the world will likely never recover.

This point, however, is critical—the condition that must be present to make it all work, a clear, comprehensible threat to our society, is in fact present. I accept that "Jihadism" is dedicated to destroy its enemies, its followers will cheerfully die for their cause, and it must be defeated. *This threat is for real and not an as-yet-to-be-revealed CIA plot as the US-hating left would have us believe.*

But, as Yogi said, "It's déjà vu all over again." *We've been there before, not long ago, and there are lessons to be learned.*

It seems eons ago yet in my post-childhood lifetime I saw the birth and death of Soviet Communism, arguably a bigger danger than Jihadism. Sadly, lessons from that showdown, so clearly part of critical evidence in today's debate, are little remembered, if at all, by many at the heart of that debate. No doubt the fact that anyone born when the Soviet Union crumbled is now twenty-five, explains that. Not many saw the entire movie. Time does fly!

In 1945, when I was fourteen, events converted a powerful scary force, Communism, into a threat to the entire planet, dividing much of the world into two hostile, highly armed blocs. It had been hoped that since Russia, a threat since 1917, had joined the "good guys" against Hitler, Russian leaders, and the quasi-religion of World Communism, could be "dealt with". This was not to be. At the close of WWII in 1945, the scales fell from our eyes as we saw the Red Army not just liberate Eastern Europe but also keep it. Everywhere the Soviet Union touched was under immediate threat. The game had changed and the first pitch, a fastball down the middle, had been thrown.

When I was sixteen, Winston Churchill made his famous

"Iron Curtain" speech and was proved right the following year when the Red Army blocked Allied access to Berlin and the famous Berlin Airlift started. When I was eighteen, Russia got the Atomic Bomb, thus the Nuclear Age was launched, while in the same year China fell to the communists, shattering forever US illusions about peace through friendly dialogue let alone nineteenth century diplomacy. If a further dose of reality were needed, the following June North Korea, egged on by Russia, invaded the South, and the Korean War was on.

By 1952, when I was twenty-one, the "West" faced a highly motivated, disciplined force that controlled much of the world and made no bones about considering itself entitled to at least dominance of the rest. *The similarity of Jihadism today to World Communism then is eerie.* As in 1952, how we got here is an accumulation of history, yet it seemed so sudden. As in 1952, a clash between civil liberties and a perceived need to act quickly and decisively shot to the surface; the issues, arguments, rhetoric, passion, philosophical debates, and deep divisions of opinion are precisely the same today as then.

In 1952, Senator Joseph McCarthy, a minor senator claiming the nickname "tail gunner Joe", who never fired a shot in anger, a drunken demagogue, a self appointed defender of liberty, waved lists of alleged spies and traitors in the US State Department without ever naming a name, and terrified a nation into believing that its government crawled with communist traitors. He accused President Truman and the hugely respected George C. Marshall of treason. Because of fears he raised, thousands lost their jobs as having suspect loyalties and thousands more were refused work. Loyalty oaths were administered by compulsion or irresistible pressure around the country. Citizen informed on citizen, friend on friend, family member on family member. Passports were withdrawn and denied arbitrarily. The FBI under J. Edgar Hoover was a force unto itself. Arbitrary arrests abounded. The country seethed with suspicion. No politician, from the President down, dared speak out against this man—to defend oneself was an admission of guilt. A wise person just kept his head down.

This was *America*, founded in liberty with what is acknowledged widely as the finest constitution in history. At the pinnacle was the Supreme Court, ever jealous of the rights of the citizen to free speech and freedom to assemble. And these weren't just bits of pretty paper—liberty, free speech, and associated rights were deeply burned into the conscience of the nation. In the United States of America, when I was twenty-one, they had free speech. So said all of them. And so it most certainly appeared to be. Until "tail gunner Joe" came along.

Under McCarthy's influence, a powerful Committee on Un-American Activities worked overtime shovelling out subpoenas demanding citizens prove their loyalty under oath. Many who lied wouldn't appear on principle or refused to answer and went to prison. Particularly hard hit was the entertainment industry, which tends toward "liberal" and hundreds were blacklisted from work. As famous actor Humphrey Bogart said, "All you had to have done was scratch your ass during the playing of the national anthem ..."

No one would challenge McCarthy, not his colleagues, not the media, not even President Eisenhower whose vice-president, later twice elected president, Richard Nixon, supported him. So, at least by strong inference, did Ronald Reagan. Congress, like our Parliament, protectors of citizens' rights, couldn't take them away fast enough. *The defender against tyranny provided not only the tyranny but the tyrant.*

It took a brave Counsel Joseph Welch, in the famous Army Hearings of 1954, finally to face McCarthy publicly, after he accused George Marshall of treason, asking, "Senator, have you left no sense of decency?" plus CBS's redoubtable Edward R. Murrow in a hard-hitting series, to finally bring this rotten bastard to his knees. The Senate, finally, though reluctantly, censured "tail gunner Joe" who died shortly afterward of extreme alcoholism, a lonely, beaten, and utterly ruined man. *Sic transit gloria.*

We're talking one man here, an undistinguished junior senator from a small state, Wisconsin, with no organization or background, who all but destroyed the civil liberties of the World's Most Powerful Nation, playing to the cheap seats with cries of fear based upon his turbid and evil imagination—one man!

But, of course, it can't happen here. This isn't 1952. Things are different. Stephen Harper is not Joe McCarthy. And he's held firmly in check by a House of Commons that protects our solid democracy from tyranny. Our Members of Parliament can be depended upon to put the rights of citizens ahead party discipline. Nowadays you can trust people in charge like the RCMP and CSIS not to be evil. And the powerful media will be ever vigilant to keep careful watch on the authorities and, if wrong is done, instantly expose it, let the chips fall where they may. Canada is different.

And pigs can fly.

FREE SPEECH

It is easy to believe in freedom of speech for those with whom we agree.
– Leo McKern

Freedom of the press is guaranteed only to those who own one.
– A. J. Liebling

My generation was raised on the notion of a free press by wartime promises. Unlike our parents, we were a naïve lot. But after all, the newspaper was the principal source of news. We knew about wartime censorship and assumed that once the war was over a free press would blossom.

Freedom of the press, or the media, is one of the basic indicia of a free society, guaranteed by constitutional imprimatur throughout the world's democracies. But it's always been on a flimsy foundation. As early as 1798, the US Congress passed the Alien and Sedition Acts, the latter of which, the Sedition Act, passed on July 14, declared that, "Any treasonable activity, including the publication of 'any false, scandalous and malicious writing,' was a high misdemeanour, punishable by fine and imprisonment." By virtue of this legislation twenty-five men, most of them editors of Republican opposition newspapers, were arrested and their newspapers forced to shut down for criticizing the President, then prosecuted on demand of that President. Here was the ridiculous and appalling situation where a revolutionary, John Adams, who had risked his life for freedom of speech and freedom of the press, now the second president of the United States, was jailing dissident newspapermen who criticized him!

I think one can make this sweeping statement—there has never been a government that hasn't tried to censor or at least limit freedom of the press and not an "establishment" that didn't support censorship.

Is there freedom of speech in Canada today? Is there censorship?

I'll relate two personal experiences and let you decide. (You must understand that Canadian journalism schools rely on the mainstream press for much of their funding.)

A few years ago I was called by a young lady who was editor of the *Annual* for Ryerson School of Journalism (one of the top if not the top school of journalism in the country). She asked me to do the principal article, which I was pleased to do, gratis.

I wrote on "free speech" and traced it back to the likes of John Wilkes, Tom Paine, and Thomas Jefferson. I closed by saying that all young people going into journalism in Canada will find that they will have to self-censor or be censored by the outlet simply not publishing the work.

Some weeks later, this young woman phoned and apologized for not getting to me earlier but she was too embarrassed. You see, I was told, my article was considered “unsuitable”.

“Was it badly written?” I asked.

“Not at all, it was very well written but just ‘unsuitable’.”

“Unsuitable to whom and on what basis?”

No answer. She then said I had two options—they would pay me $100 or I could do another, more “suitable” column.

“No.” I said, there’s another option … “You can all go fuck yourselves.”

It’s hard to imagine better proof of my views on freedom of the press!

It got better yet.

In the fall of 2011, Ryerson (short memories!) asked me to say what was my biggest disappointment in my media career. They were doing a survey.

I replied, “Having my article for Ryerson’s *Annual* rejected because it supported Free Speech.”

The lady sent me a letter saying that their rejection of my current suggestion had nothing to do with our previous contretemps. Of course not, what would make her think that I thought such a thing?

She cancelled our appointment saying my reply was—here comes that word again, folks—“unsuitable” because they were looking for disappointments of a different sort!

Closer to home, in 2000 I was "roasted" with the proceeds going to a scholarship, in my name, at the UBC School of Journalism. Billionaire Jimmy Pattison generously topped up the prize and while it's certainly not a big deal it's about $1,000 to the winner. I was asked to make the first annual presentation and say a few words. I did and repeated my admonition that they would either self-censor or be censored.

I've never been invited back.

My own scholarship!

Freedom of the press? Yeah ... right.

THE MONARCHY

The monarchy is finished. It was finished a while ago, but they're still making the corpses dance.

– Sue Townsend, author of the Adrian Mole books

As I write this, the monarchy and its suitability for Canada is much in the news as Prime Minister Harper has restored the world "Royal" to the Armed Forces. Glamour has been restored to the rather tattered image of the Royal family by Prince William marrying the beautiful Kate with now yet another two Royal brats, plus the well publicized, and distinguished military career of Harry.

For all that, compared to yesteryear, Canadians seem blasé if not bored by the Royal Family, raising the question—can, and will, the monarchy survive in Canada?

I recently read William Shawcross' *Queen Elizabeth: The Queen Mother* and that took some effort I can tell you—over 900 pages of mostly inconsequential anecdotes. It all has the aura of Hollywood and few took it too seriously.

But I remember when Royalty was a big deal, even in Quebec.

As previously mentioned, I saw George VI and Elizabeth when they were in Vancouver in May 1939 buttering up the colonials in preparation for yet another war "at Britain's side, whate'er betide" as the words of "O Canada" went in those days. And when war broke out it was "For King and Country" all over again. "God Save the King" was played at the end, and often the beginning as well, of all movies, plays, and sporting events. If "The King" was played on the radio at home, we all stood up. That's all gone now.

When, in 1937, King Edward VIII (known to his family as David) abdicated in favour of his brother Bertie (George VI) it was because he was bedding down a twice-divorced American and wanted to make it legal. What was astonishing is that while the torrid affair between "David" and Wallis was ongoing and published in papers all over the world, not a word was breathed about it in the English media—in Scotland, yes, but not England! Talk about self-censorship! It would make tears of admiration come to the eyes of Postmedia and other media published and broadcast here in Canada.

The Abdication Crisis almost ended Churchill's career as he defended the King and his right to be treated fairly. He did one last favour for his King—he wrote his brilliant abdication speech. Churchill was shouted down in the House of Commons and it became one of the principal complaints made about him on 10 May 1940 when Chamberlain recommended him to George VI as his next prime minister.

Edward was not a man overburdened with gratitude or sensitivity.

In the summer of 1940 when Churchill had his hands full with Hitler and the Luftwaffe, Edward, now the Duke of Windsor, who had become quite cozy with the Nazis, was lobbying to have his wife styled Her Royal Highness and wanted a warship to bring them home from France—just the sort of agro Churchill needed at this point in time.

Edward was banished to the Bahamas as governor; he immediately wanted to make a special visit to New York City. Again, just what Churchill needed and Edward was told that under no circumstances was he to do that and he was to stay put in Nassau or else. All this plus his cozying up to the Nazis had the Monarchy in trouble.

George VI and Elizabeth untarnished the silverware with a first-class war record. At the height of the Blitz (Buckingham Palace sustained relatively minor damage), the Queen was asked why her two daughters were not evacuated from London to the country. The Queen stated that they would not leave London unless she did, that she would not leave unless the King did, and she couldn't foresee any circumstances where he would leave his post.

The Queen—as did Churchill—often visited bombed out neighbourhoods as morale builders and it's perhaps of interest that Hitler never did. In all events the monarchy came through the war with flying colours, which is more than you can say for Churchill and the Empire.

The first few years after the end of the war Britain suffered "austerity"—added to vicious winter weather—and it must be said that when Princess Elizabeth fell in love (at any rate, we were told she did) with her handsome distant cousin Philip, there was great joy at this marvellous distraction. When in 1952 the King died of lung cancer—he was a very heavy smoker—there was genuine grief throughout the UK and in Canada. He had conquered a bad stammer, had taken over with no prior warning or preparation and to the extent Kings did things, he did them well. There is no doubt that he was loved and respected.

The movie, *The King's Speech* is, of course, a wonderful film though I don't understand how it styled German's Foreign Minister as *Count* Von Ribbentrop when he wasn't even entitled to "von" much less "Count". Although the speech that begat the movie was very special, perhaps King George is better remembered for his speech on 25 December 1939, which we all listened to on the CBC and all were puzzled to hear him quote from a poem by Minnie Louise Haskins that became so famous and caused such a stir. It's hard to understand why except perhaps at this first wartime Christmas something else was expected.

Here it is:

"I said to the man who stood at the gate of the year
'Give me a light that I may tread safely into the unknown.'
And he replied,
'Go out into the darkness and put your hand into the hand of God.
That shall be to you better than light and safer than a known way!'

So, I went forth, and finding the Hand of God,
Trod gladly into the night
He led me towards the hills
And the breaking of day in the lone east.
So, heart, be still!
What need our little life,
Our human life, to know
If God hath comprehension?
In all the dizzy strife of things
Both high and low,
God hideth his intention."

After the war, when Edward and Wallis were quite forgotten, Princess Margaret (Margaret Rose when I was a child), who had been shattered by her father's untimely death, fell in love with a divorced man sixteen years her senior—Battle of Britain veteran, Group Captain Peter Townsend, starting the Monarchy on another downhill slide. Margaret was not to get anything close to a free ride from the media.

As in 1936, the Church of England refused to countenance the marriage of an heir to the Throne to a divorced man. Queen Mary had recently died, and the Queen was about to be crowned and had planned a six-month tour of the Commonwealth. She asked her sister to postpone the matter a year. The British Cabinet refused to approve the marriage, and newspapers reported that the marriage was "unthinkable". The final blow came when Churchill, back in office, informed the Queen that the Commonwealth prime ministers were unanimously against the marriage, that Parliament would not approve a marriage, and that it would not be recognized by the Church of England unless Margaret renounced her right of succession. At the same time, polls run by popular newspapers showed considerable support for the matter to be left up to Margaret regardless of Church teaching or the government's opinion.

For two years, the matter swirled about until finally Margaret stated, "I would like it to be known that I have decided not to marry Group Captain Peter Townsend ... mindful of the Church's teachings that Christian marriage is indissoluble, and conscious of my duty to the Commonwealth, I have resolved to put these considerations before others. I have reached this decision entirely alone ..." It's perhaps nasty to note that in time Margaret overcame her blind obedience to the Church's teachings on matrimony.

The media, in stark contrast to the Edward VIII matter, had a field day with poor Margaret, and British royalty was never the same again. The genie was out of the bottle and the Royal Family, but for the Queen herself, were reduced to the level of movie stars. It became obvious to many—at least to me at any rate—that for the Royal Family to have the stature it once enjoyed, it would have to be without the constant and intimate probing of the press and that clearly wasn't going to happen. As three of her children were divorced the Queen was constantly being humiliated without the opportunity of fighting back. Rumours spread about possible infidelities of Prince Philip and she could only bite her tongue. All this brought the Queen to where she became one of the world's most admired people and for good reason, which simply highlighted the inability of her eldest son to take her place.

In the meantime the Monarchy as an institution, though perhaps not the Queen herself, became steadily less relevant in Canada. This has a great deal to do with immigrants arriving with little if any royalist feelings and the Quiet Revolution in Quebec. As Canada became more and more introspective and concerned about national unity, the monarchy lost relevance. With the possible exception of the aging Monarchist League and the aged Imperial Order of the Daughters of the Empire (IODE), the British connection means little to most Canadians, a condition sped along by the fading of British world power and influence. Such enthusiasm as remains will surely vanish when the Queen goes, for all the Throne has going for it is dignity, possessed in abundance by Her Majesty, but not much by her children.

Australia had a referendum on the monarchy and it barely hung on, but here a referendum isn't sufficient.

In Canada, interestingly enough, to abolish the monarchy under the Constitution means that all the provinces must agree, so the institution having drifted into near oblivion will be kept alive, barely, by life support from Canada's constitution. As St Paul observed, "There's a season for everything" and one must assume that that means the monarchy in Canada as well.

VE DAY FIFTY YEARS ON—WHAT A DAY!

God bless you all. This is your victory! It is the victory of the cause of freedom in every land. In all our long history we have never seen a greater day than this. Everyone, man or woman, has done their best. Everyone has tried. Neither the long years, nor the dangers, nor the fierce attacks of the enemy, have in any way weakened the independent resolve of the British nation. God bless you all.

– Winston Churchill, 8 May 1945

The most memorable years of my youth came during World War II. I was between the ages of eight and fourteen, growing up, learning, watching, and marvelling at the world around me while still often being a little boy playing little boys' games. I was a precocious youngster wanting to understand and participate in grown-up things, while on the other hand I was a little boy as well, wanting to do little boys' things.

One day I remember with great particularity was VE Day, 8 May 1945, when Germany surrendered and for a moment much of the world, including Vancouver, went mad. My father took us all downtown and it was indeed a madhouse. Rolls of toilet paper were thrown out of office windows. Anyone in a uniform seemed to be kissing a girl—in fact, you didn't have to be in uniform. Booze flowed like water. I often wonder how many babies were born nine months later!

In 1995, it was the fiftieth anniversary of VE Day, and Wendy and I decided to celebrate it in London. This is the story of that visit.

Many entertainers kept spirits up during World War II. One thinks of Bob Hope, Glenn Miller, and from Britain, George Formby and Gracie Fields. But to me the greatest of them all was Vera Lynn, the "Sweetheart of the Armed Forces".

Vera Lynn, as I write this, is ninety-eight, and recently saw a compilation of her songs go to the top of the charts in Britain, the oldest entertainer to do so, by far, in history. I'm old enough to remember her singing songs like "We'll Meet Again" (her biggest hit), "The White Cliffs of Dover", and "There'll Always be an England". I have everything she ever recorded. I also had the great luck to interview Dame Vera in 1994 just before Remembrance Day—more about that in a moment. First, let me tell you what happened to Wendy and me when we went to London on 8 May 1995, to help celebrate the fiftieth anniversary of VE Day. And what a day it was!

In London at the same time was a former law partner of mine, and long-time friend, the late Stan Winfield, who had been there on the real VE day. We all decided to go down to Buckingham Palace for the re-enactment of the Balcony scene where King George, Queen Elizabeth, Princesses Elizabeth and Margaret Rose (as she was known in those days), and Winston Churchill waved to the crowd.

The re-enactment was a pageant as only the British can do pageants, and was punctuated by a flyover of a squadron of Spitfires and Hurricanes, the backbone of the Battle of Britain in 1940 when Churchill immortalized the RAF, saying, "Never in the field of combat has so much been owed by so many to so few." Of course, the King and Churchill had long since passed on.

After the ceremony, the three of us walked down Buckingham Palace Road to find a pub. We were saying how wonderful it would have been if God had permitted Churchill to appear on that balcony for just this occasion. Just then a man came out of the crowd and went over to Stan and said, "I see by your medals you're Canadian; I'm Winston Churchill and here are my sons Jack and Randolph." Jack was named after Winston Senior's much loved brother, Randolph, after his son, Winston II's father.

It was, of course, the great man's grandson and at the time an MP. It was eerie. In fact, I had interviewed Mr. Churchill a couple of years before on a book he had written. But in light of what we had been saying it sent a shiver down the spine. He has now passed on.

That night Wendy and I went to Speakers Corner in Hyde Park for the big celebration. We had wisely purchased tickets to the stands, which held, perhaps, 3,000 people, but the entire area had some 250,000 people watching on closed circuit TV. The theme was London theatre over the years but was punctuated with World War II throwbacks. The Queen came and lit a torch, Vera Lynn sang, and it was a great night.

We were sitting next to a group of East Enders who had brought a picnic basket complete with wine and they had a marvellous time, as we did watching them. The East End of London was where Londoners were hit hardest during the "blitz". Robert Hardy, of *All Creatures Great and Small* fame, is a Churchillian and he came out to do Churchill's speech on VE Day. You could have heard a pin drop. As he intoned, *"Never in our long history have we seen a day like this ..."* he paused and at that very moment one of the East Ender ladies next to us jumped up, shook her clenched fist, and sang out, "And we stood alone!", referring to the year between June 1940 and June 1941 when Britain stood alone against the Axis. Like everyone there, of course, we shivered and tears came to our eyes.

Vera Lynn sang three songs that night but the climax came with the song that ended the night—"We'll Meet Again". 250,000 throats sang with her and there wasn't a dry eye in the house!

Later in the vacation, after visiting Blenheim Palace where Churchill was born, Wendy and I went to St Martin's parish church in the village of Bladon, near Blenheim, to see where Churchill is buried beside his beloved Clemmie and other Churchills. The grave was covered with flowers and attached to one bouquet was a note from a Dutch couple, which simply said, "Thank you for saving our country." Again we wept, especially since it was Canadian troops who liberated Holland—something the Dutch will never forget. Indeed they observe the day they were liberated every year and every school child learns about the Canadian liberation.

There's an amusing story involved. A couple of days before the Liberation, Vancouverite and later BC Lieutenant-Governor Henry Bell-Irving joined the Canadians after commanding troops in Italy. He saw two days of fighting in Holland yet got to lead the victory parade. "Budge" Bell-Irving loved to tell people about this, with a chuckle ...

Needless to say, Churchill was somehow in the air all around us, wherever we went, and as we walked out of the graveyard we met a lady with a baby in a pram.

I looked down at the child and said, "It's true, every baby looks like Winston Churchill."

The lady said, "Well he should, since his name is Winston Churchill." No relation.

I looked up to the sky and said, "Enough already, Sir Winston, enough!"

S'true, every word of it, and Wendy who is more spiritual than I simply said, "His spirit is with us," and I was in no position to argue.

Back to Vera Lynn, the "Sweetheart of the Armed Forces".

In 1994 she came to BC for the Remembrance Day services and I was privileged to interview her. What a lovely soul. The crowning moment came at the end when I had arranged that "We'll Meet Again" would be played. Off air, of course, I joined in with Dame Vera and sang along with her with tears streaming down my face.

This was my happiest broadcasting moment—by far.

SUDDENLY!

Racism springs from the lie that certain human beings are less than fully human. It's a self-centred falsehood that corrupts our minds into believing we are right to treat others as we would not want to be treated.

– Alveda King, NAACP member, minister, civil rights leader, niece of Martin Luther King

We've changed, oh my, have we changed and so very quickly.

When I was a child, Indians were seen as shiftless drunks, usually found in "beer parlours" or passed out outside. Whites were contemptuous of them. No one had a good word for them; no one was on their side except a few bleeding hearts and their lawyers.

In school, I learned about Iroquois, Huron, and Algonquin but nothing of tribes in BC. It was a void. My ignorance carried on until fairly recent times. My observations tell me, however, that I reflected the views of other British Columbians generally who were, like me, moving—at a glacial pace, perhaps—toward a better understanding of what aboriginal peoples stood for and what they meant to our overall community.

It was amazing, when you think about it. It isn't as if the aboriginals weren't there. Of course they were, as much as they are now. The problem was they were simply ignored by the European society and treated as if they didn't exist. There were special laws respecting their obligations not to drink off the reservation and things of that nature and special laws to "protect" their way of life.

Without doubt, alcoholism was a huge problem with natives. Why would that come as a surprise considering the way we had castrated their culture and hived them off from the rest of society? And "educated" them in residential schools? To their eternal credit, First Nations of themselves have done an unbelievable job in cleaning up alcoholism.

Let me give you an example of the way natives were treated.

I was once in a courtroom in Williams Lake waiting for my client's case to be called when a young aboriginal lad was brought forward charged with driving while his license was under suspension. The judge looked around the courtroom and asked if there were any members of the media there. Since I was the only one present, the answer was obviously no.

I watched as the case was presented. Apparently this lad's license had been suspended by the Superintendent of Motor Vehicles, not the court, quite a distinction as you'll see. The RCMP officer gave evidence that he had been stopped, on the reservation, and not only could not produce a driver's license but it was in fact under suspension.

Now, if the court had suspended the license, then the charge would have been contempt of court, a very serious matter. The courts do not, however, treat suspension by the superintendent nearly so seriously and usually the penalty is an extension of the suspension, a fine, or both. The judge sentenced this lad to six months in prison even though it was a first offence! I sent a report to the Attorney-General, Alex Macdonald, but heard nothing.

I could also mention the many times I watched cases with aboriginals in court in Kamloops; the common sight was Monday morning with about eight or ten of them trooping into court, holding up their pants because their belts have been taken away, and charged with common drunkenness on the reservation that past Saturday night.

It may well be that in all of these cases the natives were drunk. One had to wonder, however, why the RCMP were so diligent in patrolling *reservations* on a Saturday night and yet not diligent at all in patrolling European communities and looking for drunks there—of which I can assure you there were plenty!

Natives were badly patronized by the authorities. When I became MLA for Kamloops and a cabinet minister, there was a bridge proposed to cross the North Thompson River, the east end of which would have crossed the reservation to the Yellowhead highway. This required, of course, the use of reserve land and the cry from the talk shows was to start expropriation proceedings if the First Nations didn't promptly consent.

I got into the middle of this and said emphatically that this was not going to happen and that I would negotiate with Chief Mary Leonard and the Kamloops Indian Band and was confident I could make a deal. Told this would take too long, my reply was, "This is their land—we have to respect that." The bottom line was that Chief Leonard, the council, and I made a deal in reasonably timely fashion and both sides were satisfied. The point is, of course, that no one ever thought of doing this before.

The practical effect for me was very positive in that I was endorsed in the next election by Chief Leonard and the council and did extremely well with First Nations bands in my constituency. This was not my motive—my reason was that it was time and I was supported by my colleague Alex Fraser, Highways Minister, Alan Williams, who was in charge of Indian Affairs, and Premier Bill Bennett.

There was much more of course. I well recall a prominent businessman, a client, coming into my office one day demanding that I take action against the Kamloops Indian band for extortion. What had happened is that the band had raised the rent on beautiful lakeshore property he and his friends leased for summer homes on Paul Lake from $25 a year to $100 a year and the lessees were screaming blue murder. I looked at this man and asked him if he had lost his mind. $100 a year was "peppercorn" rent in itself and I couldn't understand how they had gotten away with such outrageous rent up until then. I told them they could find another lawyer.

I then found out that the Band wished to raise the rent substantially higher, to a reasonable market price, such as charged for similar properties at the Shuswap lakes, but that the Indian agent, appointed by the federal government and a European, "wouldn't give them permission". It was their land and they couldn't get permission!

Is it any surprise that this sort of insult pissed off First Nations?

There is of course the outrageous case of Shaughnessy Golf Club where the golf club managed to get land from the Musqueam Indian Nation sufficient for their golf course and leased land for houses at what was an outrageously low price for a ninety-nine-year lease. This, too, was approved by the Indian agent and the Department of Indian Affairs. Eventually, the Musqueam went to the Supreme Court of Canada and the whole scam was turned aside and they were awarded appropriate compensation. This sort of crap occurred all around the province for decades and the white community thought nothing of it!

In 1973, the Calder case went to the Supreme Court of Canada on the question of aboriginal right to land. The court split 3–3 and Prime Minister Trudeau decided that was enough for the federal government to enter negotiations with aboriginals over land rights and other matters.

Not everyone was pleased with this notion, least of all my friend and colleague Melvin H. Smith, QC, who wrote a book called *Our Home* Or *Native Land*. It was highly critical of the right of aboriginals to have land in their own name and I, frankly, not only agreed with him but also wrote the foreword to the book.

The matter of land rights started to get before the courts in a number of cases and decision after decision from the Supreme Court of Canada informed us of what the Constitution of Canada plainly said but we preferred not to believe. Many of us didn't much like what we were hearing. In my own case, because I'm a lawyer perhaps, eventually the light went on and I realized that it didn't much matter what any of us might have wished the Constitution to say; we had to live with it as it was and that Supreme Court of Canada decisions were the law of the land. As time went on it became pretty clear to me and I'm sure to many others that the Constitution was in fact morally right, while we had been wrong. It helped me that my classmate, Tom Berger, a man I admired enormously, was in the thick of battles on the side of natives.

As I thought about it, it was not rocket science. The Europeans had come to British Columbia and simply taken the land that they found, created their own land registry system, and Bob's your uncle. That this was not satisfactory ought to have occurred to us a long time ago but didn't. It all seemed so right; we'd conquered them, hadn't we?

In fact, we hadn't; but even if we had, modern international law doesn't regard conquest as definitive of the matter. In any event, the laws we Europeans had made bound us to adjust our views and recognize native title. We have no choice but to accept the fact we can no longer do as we please with native land or disputed land. And, in my view, that's as it should be. It's indeed remarkable that there has been such a sea change in attitudes of

Europeans. What is even more remarkable is how quickly it has happened.

In the years that followed, the Supreme Court of Canada made a number of decisions to which I have alluded. I began to change my mind simply because there was no option—I was now officially wrong in law and so was Mel. As I accepted that, I was forced to think of the justice of the situation and whether or not Europeans could take the moral ground in this debate and decided for the reasons that I have given above, that they could not.

As Emerson put it, "Foolish consistency is the hobgoblin of little minds ..."

Thus, I changed my mind substantially. I have no way of knowing what Mel Smith would've done had he lived; however, he was a practical man and I suspect that he and I would've talked it through to the conclusion that I have reached.

A MEMORABLE TEACHER

A teacher affects eternity; he can never tell where his influence stops.
– Henry Adams, American historian, son and grandson of US presidents

I don't mind learning but I don't always like being taught.
– Winston Churchill

I don't suppose anyone forgets their first teacher. Mine were the Misses Beemans (a pair of sisters) at the first kindergarten I ever attended, an experience that happened in rather a strange way.

I was four and living at 43rd and Macdonald in Kerrisdale. My best friend, Gregor Macintosh, a year older than I, had been enrolled in the Misses Beemans' kindergarten at 42nd and Macdonald so I had no one to play with. One day, my loneliness took me up to the Misses Beemans and the next thing I knew I had enrolled myself in the kindergarten! This came as a great surprise to my mother who, thinking I was missing, was in a panic but decided, before calling the police, that I might have gone to find Gregor so she came up to the Beeman sisters to see her missing son happily playing with Gregor and other newfound playmates! I was permitted to stay and now had someone to play with. And I had started my education!

My next education step was Jack and Jill Kindergarten on W45th near the Boulevard. My teachers there were Miss Haynes and Miss Shears and all I can really recall is that they were very nice and that I got gold and silver stars on my report card (good) and no blue ones (bad).

Many of the kids became lifelong friends, including a Vancouver mayor, Philip Owen, and a damned good one, whom I still call Pip; his older brother David; Molly Lou Shaw, who became my sister-in-law; and my ubiquitous cousin, Hugh. "Pip" Owen's dad was Walter S. Owen, one of my dad's best friends and later Lieutenant-Governor of the province, while his mom, Jean nee Dowler, was a very dear friend of my mom's and they were classmates at Crofton House.

I then went to Maple Grove Elementary School, just up the street, and my first teacher was Miss Dunlop. I remember her as a very kind *old* lady. About forty years later, during a radio show, I mentioned her and said, "She must be long gone by now." I received a phone call off air from a very amused Miss Dunlop who had retired just five years before! I suppose she was probably about thirty-five when I thought she was an old lady!

My Grade II teacher was a Miss Gray about whom I remember

little except that she was gentle—not a bad thing to be remembered for. My Grade III teacher, an otherwise pleasant lady, had a habit of smacking one across the back of the hand with a ruler when they misbehaved. I didn't like her much for that. I also remember Mr. Kerr, our science teacher in Grade IV who got me very interested in the subject—an interest I'm afraid I lost when Physics came along. There was some social excitement—my music teacher was a lesbian living openly with another lesbian caring not a hoot for what people thought. I didn't know that of course and just thought Miss Lawrence was a neat music teacher.

Sunday School and the church choir were a part of my life from ages six through twelve. This all took place at St Mary's, Anglican, in Kerrisdale, 37th Ave and Larch, the church where I was first married in September 1955 and where Mom's Memorial Service was held in December 1990. I don't really remember Sunday School except it was taught by a rather dour man, Mr. LeNeveau. It wasn't a whole hell of a lot of fun.

Except! One morning the seemingly mirthless LeNeveau cracked a joke (that, I think, shows that humour trumps catechisms). It seems a Sunday School teacher brought out a glass of scotch whiskey and a worm and showed them to his class. He dropped the worm in the glass and it promptly died.

"What message does that give you?" he asked his charges.

Little Johnny (somehow it's always Johnny) piped up, "If you don't want worms, drink whiskey."

After Sunday School, some of us repaired upstairs to the robing room where we donned surplices, cassocks, and a most uncomfortable, stiff, frill thing around our necks. We then joined the Senior Choir and it was time for the Sunday Morning service captained by the Reverend Dudley Kemp, an Englishman with a rare, for them, love of baseball. He was a great guy and not too hard for little boys to listen to!

At the end of the "season", summertime, we choirboys were always paid an honorarium. Hugh and I always seemed to get thirty-five cents while the stars, Ken Gunning and Philip Rive, both sadly gone now, got a dollar. They always looked so damned angelic when they sang, which pissed us off no end.

1942 saw me at the St George's school for boys. It was a classic English school with cricket and rugby the big games. The Head Master, John Harker, got apoplectic at the mere mention of Canadian football or baseball. There my first teacher was Herb Bourne, later a Catholic priest. I liked him very much even though he was the first to give me the cane. I got two strokes, one less than the usual minimum, and not very hard, because he didn't have his heart in it. I got them for sloppy writing, a habit that has followed me throughout life.

After coming first in the class at Christmas I was moved up from Grade V to Grade VI, happily joining Denis. In Grade VI, I finished fourth at the end of the year.

It was in Grade VI I was introduced to Captain B. O. Robinson, Royal Sussex Regiment, a badly wounded veteran of World War I who, amongst other things, instilled in me a love of English literature. He had never been to university and on the roster of teachers posted on the bulletin board, where others had their degrees listed, there was simply "Royal Sussex Regiment" next to which a schoolboy wag had scrawled, "Didn't he go to school?"

Cappy, as we called him, was a remarkable man. Because of his terrible war wounds, he had a vicious temper. When he lost it he became so very contrite. He lost it at me one day and sentenced me to four hours detention on Saturday morning, a punishment almost as bad as the cane. In the middle of my detention, Cappy came by and said, "Let's have some lunch and go to the rugby game." He treated me at a restaurant near the Stanley Park Entrance, which included my favourite, a chocolate sundae, and then we went to the rugby game at the Brockton Oval in Stanley Park. It was quite a feeling for a young lad.

Another time, he held a class story-writing contest. Mine was a naval story called "The Poppin Bay Mystery" for which I received first prize, a book by eighteenth-century Royal Navy officer and superb writer Captain Frederick Marryat. Sadly, I no longer have the book, which came from Cappy's own collection, and in which he had inscribed, "Well done, Mair, no wonder you want to be in the navy." When we were in Grade VII, he introduced us to Dickens and would read us a chapter of *Great Expectations* almost every day and we loved it.

Cappy was also our Latin teacher and he made that dead language come alive. I loved it. In those days there was a debate as to whether or not the Latin "V" was "hard" or "soft". He settled the issue, for me anyway, by asking, "Can you imagine Julius Caesar crossing the Rubicon and saying, 'weeny, weedy, weeky', not '*veni*, *vidi, vici*'?"

Cappy was our rugby coach and a stern one. He would run up and down the sidelines hollering, "Tackle low, chaps, tackle low," and if a chap didn't, Cappy would raise hell as only he could do. And we produced a championship team in our age group. Cappy was a stoic and, when the weather was wretched or the ground hard with frost, he would cheerfully pronounce, "It's only what your father did before you." Needless to say, it wasn't Cappy being rained on or pounded into the hard ground!

The ubiquitous Cappy was also our cricket master, a game I loved, as he did, and he would spin us yarns about his passion. One day in the practice nets he put a quarter—worth probably $5 now—on the middle wicket and dared me to knock it off. I did on the first bowl. Denis tried to convince me that I should return the money but to hell with that—I'd won it fair and square!

Captain Robinson taught us so much about London that when I first went there in 1964, I almost felt as if I'd grown up there. Cappy had two sons, one, Basil, became a very well known Ottawa civil servant, and Geoff, a top-notch orthopaedic surgeon. For all he had warts, and there were many, Captain Basil O. Robinson was the most unforgettable teacher I ever had.

TIME FOR HIGHER EDUCATION

A man who has never gone to school may steal from a freight car; but if he has a university education, he may steal the whole railroad.
– Theodore Roosevelt

My academic career at university was not something of which I am at all proud. I found when I got to the University of British Columbia that I had fallen into terrible study habits since leaving St George's in 1946. There was no one to make me study, there were plenty of neat temptations and almost no restraints.

I got through first year but second year completely did me in. I joined a fraternity, Zeta Psi, which was part of my undoing in that it gave me a place, the fraternity house with a Coke machine converted to beer, where I could go when I didn't feel like studying, which was most of the time. I also discovered, in no particular order, golf, bridge, and girls. To make a long story short, I failed the year mostly because I didn't write most of the exams. My father was more forgiving than I perhaps would have been, and I took on second year again and passed reasonably.

Third year was a pivotal year because my father had told me that either I found something to aim at or I might as well simply go out to work now. That, along with a lot of encouragement from Med McFarlane, QC, (whom we met earlier) encouraged me towards Law.

I had a problem. I had to get past French 202. I had flunked it every year mainly because I couldn't stand the class and didn't bother writing exams. Now it was essential that I get through but I finished the year not having gone to any lectures. I had decided to take it in Summer School and had already arranged to do so with Dean Walter Gage. One of the features of French 202 was a book one was required to read. I did not even know what the book for this year was.

Here came one of the many lucky breaks of my life.

On the day of the exam I was in the cafeteria with sometime girlfriend and future sister-in-law, Molly Lou Shaw, who asked me why I wasn't going to the exam. I told her that I didn't even know what the book I was required to read was so it was useless. She said, "It's *Vol De Nuit* or *Night Flight* in English, by St Éxupery, and I happen to have an English copy. Why don't you read it? It's short and very good, and then just take a shot at the exam?"

I took her advice, read the book, English copy, of course, went into the exam, and discovered to my delight and utter amazement that the first question, for 75 marks out of 150, was "Give a précis, *in English*, of *Vol de Nuit*." I couldn't believe my luck and was able to reproduce the book, virtually, and to my surprise and delight received 79 out of 150! I had passed French 202 and was on my way to the UBC School of Law!

In September 1953, I entered Law School along with ninety-nine other aspiring lawyers. At the end of third year we were down to fifty. In those days, you see, there was no LSAT and the selection process was simply failing students, mostly in first year. Brutal but effective.

I loved Law School. I found it hard work and my bad study habits put me at a disadvantage I had to quickly overcome. I was by no means a brilliant student but I did finish in the top third of the class, graduating in 1956, by which time I had a wife, Eve, and a baby son, Kenneth Rafe II.

The class of 1956 was an unusual one in that it contained a fantastic mix of guys, and gals, those who loved to drink beer and study and those who didn't, the former outnumbering the latter. Needless to say, I was an enthusiastic member of the former. We had some very interesting people including Ron Basford, who became a senior cabinet minister in the federal government, several Supreme Court judges including Tom Berger (who became an outstanding aboriginal rights lawyer), Bob Hutchison, Ken Fawcus, Nick Drossos, John Spencer, with Tom Braidwood, Harold "Bud" Hollinrake, and Duncan Shaw on the Court of Appeal. There were also a number of provincial court judges amongst us. I, of course, was BC cabinet minister. Our Gold Medalist was Rendina Hossie, and Elaine Evans was runner-up. They were not known for their beer drinking. Notwithstanding the fact that we also had a murderess, and one murdered by the "mob" for not paying gambling debts, it was a highly successful class and is looked upon as one of the best classes the Law School has produced.

I have to confess that I was not a "varsity" type. I was utterly unenthusiastic about the University of British Columbia and couldn't have cared less about such things as the "Great Trek". I never did really become involved, and, quite frankly, was delighted when I left. I realize that this is nothing to boast about and I greatly honour those graduates who supported the university while at school and later. I just was not one of them. I must say the same thing applied to Law School. Once I had left … finis. I do go to the law class reunions and enjoy myself immensely but since the next one is our sixtieth, there aren't a hell of a lot of us left.

In 2005, I received an honorary Doctor of Laws from Simon Fraser University and I must admit I am very proud of this. I can well understand why I have not been similarity honoured by UBC since I've done absolutely nothing to justify it. I had always, however, been interested in Simon Fraser University and it wasn't until I thought about it I realized why. They are rebels and the administration didn't curtail the political activity of the students. There was a ferment on the campus that I had not experienced at UBC.

I thought more about that and realized there was a very good reason. When I was at UBC it was very large, mainly because of returned veterans who brought a rather sober atmosphere to the campus and were not the sort to picket, march, or revolt against anything. They were there for an education, period. There was a sense of gravitas about the university because these veterans had come to learn, not to play, and it rubbed off on the atmosphere. I'm sure that things have changed since then! In all events, I did get my LL.B and practiced law for some fifteen years before I found honest work and went into politics!

I cannot leave this subject without observing that UBC and SFU must be the two most beautiful campuses on earth. UBC, on the Point Grey peninsula with terrific views of the outer harbour and Howe Sound; Simon Fraser, on a hill in Burnaby, has spectacular views to the North up the North Arm of Burrard Inlet and, to the South, of the Salish Sea.

I remember that a great challenge of Law School were the views from the first- and third-year classes. In second year, the hardest one, we luckily looked out at the back of the Field House.

HOW DID IT ALL TURN OUT?

You can't make positive choices for the rest of your life without an environment that makes those choices easy, natural, and enjoyable.
– Deepak Chopra

I believe that you are what your surroundings make you. There are many factors, of course, but I believe that where I grew up, the place I love so much had a profound influence on three areas of my later life—a love of writing, a love of books, and a love of the environment.

I don't say that had I been born and lived elsewhere I might not have become a writer or loved books and the environment. It would have been much different though and, after all, this is *my* story of growing up in the City of the Horse Buns in the Province of British Columbia.

Cappy gave me the love of reading and writing, my Mom the

love of reading and books, my Dad the love of the environment. These three things, in my mind, are intertwined. For example, if I had not grown up where I did, and learned to love what we now call the "environment", I might never have been so attracted to Rachel Carson's Silent Spring and not turned so much passion to "environmental" matters.

To me, British Columbia and especially my city are not easily severable, if at all, from what I am, what I have done, and why I did them and how.

Am I satisfied? Of course not. No one can be satisfied with their life no matter how long or short. There are always pluses and minuses, disgraces and accomplishments, happy days and sad days, moments of great joy, and occasions of tragedy and sorrow. All one can really do is try to be moderately happy on balance and we're very much helped by the fact that we all forget a lot more than we remember. The mind has a marvellous way of burying a lot of things that should be buried. I think it's the ability to put these things out of mind that allows one have accomplishments where, if they were remembered, moping would take the place of work. As Churchill once observed, "I've had a lot of trouble in my life, most of which didn't happen."

On balance, I'm pleased that in the last half of my life I did accomplish some things that I always wanted to do. I very much enjoyed practicing law, my life in politics, and I particularly loved my time in radio. I suppose what I am most pleased with is that I was able to make some difference with my writing. In fact, as I think about it now at eighty-three, I am most pleased that I was able to convince some people that I was able to write and, in fact, actually get paid for it.

I was very fortunate, especially in my later years. I met Wendy when I was sixty-two and it has been a marvellous love affair ever since. I was a late bloomer lucky enough to have bloomed a bit even though I was tardy about it.

Deepak Chopra is right. What you become has a lot to do with your environment and, in that regard, that's the luckiest part of my life.

ON WRITING

Writing a book is an adventure. To begin with it is a toy and an amusement. Then it becomes a mistress, then it becomes a master, then it becomes a tyrant. The last phase is that just as you are about to be reconciled to your servitude, you kill the monster and fling him to the public.

– Winston Churchill

To write, you must overcome inertia and hit that first key! That's the hard part of writing, I think. That wonderful humourist of the '30s and '40s, Robert Benchley, once said, "It took me fifteen years to discover that I had no talent for writing, but I couldn't give it up because by that time I was too famous to quit!"

Benchley became not only a famous writer but an outstanding character movie actor, a lifetime member of the "Round Table" at the Algonquin Hotel in New York and the bosom pal, if not more, of Dorothy Parker, the superb writer comedic genius, and, along with Alexander Woolcott, the soul of the Round Table. Woolcott was, incidentally, the inspiration for the great play, *The Man Who Came To Dinner*, written by George Kaufman and Moss Hart, starring Monty Woolley, which Mom took me to when I was about twelve. Kaufman was a regular at the Round Table as was, of course, Woolcott, while Woolley and Hart were "sometimers".

A few years ago, Wendy and I splurged and spent three days at the Algonquin to soak up the atmosphere. The great characters are all gone, of course; there is no more Round Table luncheon group, but the table is still there and so, palpably, is the atmosphere. And, as in days of yore, a cat. The Algonquin was money well spent. Coming from my mom, I have long been a fan of Benchley, Dorothy Parker, Woolcott, Edna Ferber, George Kaufman, and the lot. *The New Yorker* magazine, the genius Harold Ross's baby, which he nurtured into a grand adulthood, was an early and constant read of mine and, amongst other things, spawned a lifetime love of cartoons. I remember, probably starting in my early teens, if not before, laughing at Helen Hockinson, Peter Arno, Charles Adams, James Thurber, and so many others.

Far from being in Benchley's league, I still find that a healthy part of my income over the years came from writing—in fact most of it, if you count editorials I did on radio for nearly twenty-five years.

Not long ago, I came across my old 1949 High School Annual and was astonished to find I wrote seven articles plus the music page in the school paper. It's all pretty dull stuff but, there I was, a writer. Later, in third-year Law, I wrote a case review for the *UBC*

Legal Notes (now *The Law Review*), which was the first time I was officially published. It was an honour and I'm proud of it.

I did zilch from then until 1975 when, as MLA for Kamloops, I wrote monthly columns for the *Kamloops Sentinel* and the *Kamloops News*—for whom I later wrote a regular column. With the exception of one done after a visit to Hiroshima, which makes me weep when I read it today, these columns were typical politician's bullshit—but I did have a byline.

Around that time I spoke with the sainted Bruce Hutchison and asked him for advice. He said, "Rafe, a column should have a beginning, a middle, and an end with some words that show some degree, however tenuous, of continuity." That's all I can say for my writing at its best! I've tried, with admittedly limited success, to follow Bruce's advice. (Incidentally, Bruce's son Bob, who became Mr. Justice Robert Hutchison, was a classmate in that wonderful Class of 1956.)

My first professional column was in 1981 for the *Financial Post*, as it then was, for which I wrote off and on, mostly on, until 2001 when Conrad Black bought the paper and I was gracelessly informed of my leave-taking by having my column returned with a note saying it was no longer required. Contrary to industry practice, the bastards didn't even pay me a "spike" fee. Real classy! I was annoyed because Diane Francis, my editor, was a friend and fun to write for. Unhappily, the media is not known for class.

In the late '80s, while writing for Diane, I was offered a column in the *Globe and Mail* by an editor, Sarah Murdoch, for a little bit more than I was getting at the *FP*. I was quite flattered. When

I told Diane she became quite upset and called the *Globe* "those fellatio performers", or words to that effect, and asked, "What will they pay you, $50 more a column? I'll raise yours $75." In fact, they only offered me $25 more but Diane left no time to answer her question, so I "reluctantly" accepted the raise. I said, "I'm glad someone loves me." The next morning a huge bouquet of flowers arrived at the radio station with a card saying, "We love you." It was the high water mark of my writing career and I get quite a charge of being able to say that I turned down a column with "Canada's National Newspaper", the reason, incidentally, you may find interesting.

I couldn't have done the *Globe* column anyway. Sarah wanted me to do a column called "The West". I told her that I didn't live in "The West" but on the Pacific Coast and that I had no idea what people in the Prairie Provinces thought about current affairs or what their concerns were and that it would be very wrong of me to pretend to speak for them. I had not been to many of the population centres and the larger ones I had only visited once or twice. I believed, as I believe now, that my trying to speak on behalf of the Prairies would be the equivalent of somebody from Winnipeg writing on behalf of the people of BC. This was simply beyond her comprehension—her view was the traditional one that the "West" began at the Manitoba border with Ontario and from there to the west coast everyone was a "westerner".

I wrote for *Equity Magazine*, which sadly went under. The owner, the late Harvey Southam of the famous journalism family, was a gem to write for, as was his editor, Charlie Smith, for whom I later wrote at the *Georgia Straight* where he's still editor and not looking a day older.

I wrote a few columns for Stevie Cameron's late and much lamented *Elm Street*. I scribbled a column for the *Vancouver Courier* in two separate relationships, loved them, and left on the best of terms both times, and for the *Georgia Straight* and ditto my leaving them for one of my two stints at the *Courier*. The *Now* papers fired me because my columns weren't political enough! I was fired by a family magazine whose name I've forgotten—actually they went belly up so perhaps that wasn't a firing after all though they sure framed it that way—and I wrote for the *David Black* community papers for several years. They definitely fired me on purely political grounds because they were hard "right" and I wasn't. In fact, I had been warned about my "wet" opinions. I was also fired by the *North Shore Outlook*.

The *Vancouver Province* hired me to do a weekly column on "anything I wished", which I did for several months until the editor who had hired me, Michael Browne, moved on. There was considerable tension thereafter between my new editor and me—her idea of the suitability of "anything I wished" and mine differed dramatically. I had the pleasure of actually publicly firing the *Province* because they had censored Gordon Gibson and I despise all manner of censorship.

After I left 600AM in 2005, I began writing for *The Tyee*, thetyee.ca, under the editorship of the estimable David Beers who, like me, had taken his lumps in the mainstream media. At this writing, nearly ten years later, our relationship remains excellent.

I've had to change the syntax once in a while and be brought up short on possible libel but I've had a completely free hand with the content.

Unhappily, not long after I wrote this, Dave was no longer my editor, and was replaced by one Jane Armstrong. I sensed I was not long for this world almost from the moment she got involved. After a long life and many firings, I knew what these things felt like!

She started to edit my pieces for "politically correct" language and for matters of style she felt that she could do better. The stated cause of my dismissal, after column number four, was "plagiarism" and I cannot imagine a more terrible thing to say to a writer unless it was true.

Here's what had happened—the reader can judge. I had used a paragraph in a proposed article for *The Tyee*, which I had written and had published in *The Common Sense Canadian* for which I write and am a co-founder. I rather liked the phrasing and, after all, I had written it—they were my words.

I submitted the article to Armstrong on 6 March 2015 and she replied, "Rafe, the above sentence is identical to a passage in the *Vancouver Observer* Feb. 16, 2015. Please reword to avoid plagiarism allegation."

I immediately replied, "I said it before, in the *Observer,* in the *Common Sense Canadian*, and repeated it because it has it been challenged, *they plagiarized my article of January as did several other papers.*" (Emphasis in original correspondence to Armstrong.)

Armstrong apparently chose to ignore this absolute defence

and fired me. I bear no grudge—I don't do well with that anyway—and prefer to remember nearly eleven years helping David Beers get *The Tyee* up, running, and successful.

I then briefly wrote for Linda Solomon Wood at the *National Observer*, an online paper associated with the *Vancouver Observer.* One of her editors tried to rewrite my column—literally—and substitute his opinion on Constitutional matters for mine. Since I have a wealth of experience, at the highest level in this subject, and he, an American has none I quit. I suspect that because the article was somewhat uncomplimentary to Central Canada, and the *National Post* had just started in Toronto, well ... you get my drift.

I also write for the environmental group Damien Gillis and I started, *The Common Sense Canadian*, thecommonsensecanadian.com, and for my own website, rafeonline.com. *Common Sense*, incidentally, refers to the famous pamphlet, indeed the inspiration of The American Revolution, "Common Sense" by Thomas Paine of whom Damien and I are great admirers.

For several years I wrote twice monthly for the *Strategic Culture Foundation*, a Russian online paper. They recruited me after reading my website and I wrote about one Canadian's view of World Affairs. I was under no constraints and criticism of Russia was quite acceptable. Then Vladimir Putin tightened his grip, and the ugly hand of censorship tightened too. Soon Russia became out of bounds, then the Middle East, and then I left. Sadly it's now a government organ.

I have published twelve books at this writing and if you're reading this, make that a baker's dozen. My first was on fly-fishing and most of the rest political exercises. I don't pretend to even be a good writer—I can say that it has made me a decent living mostly on a small local stage. But I love it, and isn't that pretty important?

WHITHER THE BOOK?

I would be most content if my children grew up to be the kind of people who think decorating consists mostly of building enough bookshelves.
– Anna Quindlen

Like the drunk of yesteryear, I should be interdicted against going into my version of the boozer—the bookstore.
– Rafe Mair

For my pre-TV generation, books were hugely important. Everyone I knew read. Moreover, Vancouver was a hotbed of very good writers. I cut my teeth on the truly great Jack Scott of the *Vancouver Sun* and the internationally acclaimed humourist, Eric Nicol of the *Province*. There was Barry Mather of the *News Herald* and later the *Vancouver Sun*. (Mather, looking at the "clubs" we had before cocktail lounges, observed that "the Pacific Athletic Club is no more noted for athletes than the Arctic Club is for

Eskimos.") Outdoors folks had two first-class writers in Mike Cramond of the *Province* and Lee Straight of the *Sun* and always around with world-class outdoors literature was Roderick Haig-Brown of Campbell River. Sports had Eric Whitehead and Clancy Loranger, both fine and amusing penmen. Whitehead started every baseball season with an article on "Detroit's annual run for the pennant". Jim Taylor, the late Jim Kearney, and other good ones came along but I cannot forget the very fine "owner" of the second front page of the *Sun*, after Jack Wasserman and Allan Fotheringham, the late Denny Boyd, who started with the *Sun* in Sports. And of course there was Bruce Hutchison, of whom even Ontario had heard.

With modern technology, are books now doomed to be curiosities in an antique store along with coal oil lamps and ear trumpets? Does anyone give a damn?

They well might be doomed with the advent of the e-book accessing hundreds of thousands of books and cheaply. Most classics of yesteryear are in the public domain and are all available online—often free! It's not easy to compete with free. But I have hope. Books have a long history, though that didn't help the bow and arrow, the spear, or the horse.

Until the fifteenth century, books were primitive, fragile, and reserved for the powerful. This changed when the Gutenberg press arrived in 1450 CE, having an enormous impact on the Renaissance and the Reformation, giving a boost for the former and being the principal catalyst of the latter. In this man's opinion, the printing press was the biggest historical boon to communications prior to the arrival of the computer. Before, with books handwritten on parchment, communication in any real sense rested with those who could read and write, meaning the "Upper Class" and especially the church. (The phrase "benefit of clergy" meant someone who was a priest, thus able to read and write. It now, apparently, in the negative, refers to unwed couples.) Books then became more widely available and all that was needed was a literate public—and that would happen by reason of the new availability of books—it was a fifteenth-century version of "build it and they will come". Who would dare hazard a guess as to how many books have been published since 1450 CE and how many people have read how many words? Books are deeply imbedded in our lives and indeed culture, but is that sufficient for their survival?

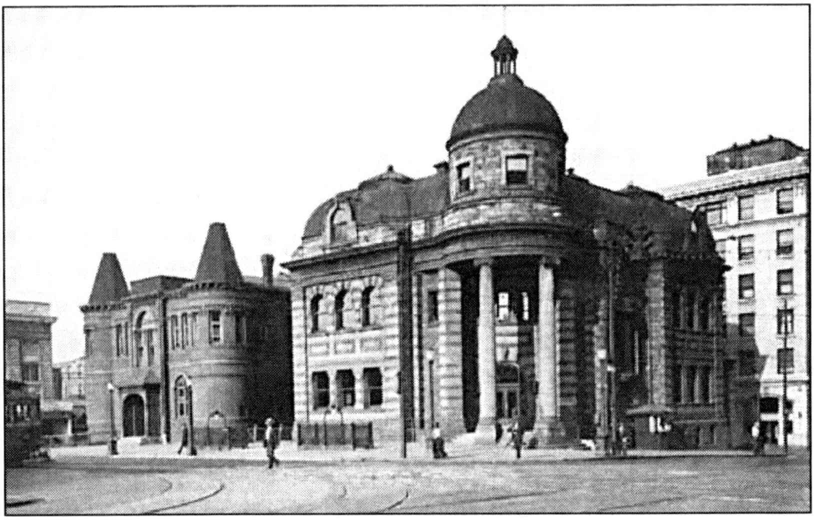

Vancouver Public Library, Main and Hastings, ca 1910.
Donated by Andrew Carnegie, still there, may the saints be praised, as The Carnegie Community Centre

I grew up in a family of readers, especially my mother. Not only did Mom read *to* me and then *with* me, she, whether by design or accident, always left good reading material lying around the house. I became a reader, then a buyer of books so that Wendy and I, somehow in our small townhouse, have over 3,000 books.

As mentioned earlier, my great teacher, Captain Robinson, had a lot to do with my love of not only reading and writing but of the books themselves. The atmosphere of his class in English literature was more than just memorizing poems or interpreting paragraphs and a lot more to do with the whole story of the printed book. He once likened a book to a lovely willow, properly crafted, cricket bat. Of course it should perform but how much better the performance felt if the bat itself oozed character.

I love books for their own sake—I like the heft and feel. I love the look of them and rejoice in their possession even if they remain unread for quite a time. In that respect they're like a stamp collection—you don't have to look at them all the time to revel in their ownership.

I'm not well read because I concentrate on personal preferences, not on what would make me a well-rounded reader. I tend to read history, politics, international affairs, and biographies; Wendy does social issues and reads fiction, which I only do rarely. I should read more fiction and I know it. I keep up on social issues by listening to her. We talk books a lot.

I worry for the small independent bookseller. In that regard I'm a Luddite, wishing to destroy the big-time publishers and the computer fiends that supply them. And I'll be no more successful than those who smashed the machines of the Industrial Revolution. I'm cheered, however, by the fact that many artisans survived the Industrial Revolution and niche opportunities cropped up. So it may well be with the book.

My fears are for the small bookseller like my bookstore, 32 Books in Edgemont Village, North Vancouver, who are hanging in there nicely by super service and broadening the products they offer. My habit is to case the shelves of Indigo Chapters and take my selections to 32 Books for ordering if they're not in stock, which they often are. I must, in truth, admit to using Amazon but especially, for used books, Abe.com.

It does no good to gnash one's teeth and even less to pretend, as radio lovers did with television, that the crisis will go away. It won't, if only because there's a new generation out there that was born into the digital world and has no sense of nostalgia for days past. Moreover, they can read off a screen, something us old-timers have trouble with. I, for example, must print out my writings and edit hard copy in a font and size I can read. (Shush up—I know that my editing still leaves much to be desired.)

In all this pessimism I hold out hope for the small bookstore, new and used, for they are more than just stores. In the same way that the technology has long been available to buy groceries online, people like markets. They love to congregate, window shop, and have coffee and muffins. They go to many stores to meet friends and talk with the shopkeeper. That is especially so with small bookstores.

As I write this, in late 2014, the statistics show that sales of e-books have flattened and that there is renewed confidence in the traditional book. Bookstores are reviving somewhat and there is hope that a workable level has been found. I "collect" used bookstores like those in Hay-on-Wye on the Welsh-England border and Wigtown in Scotland, both of which have many such stores; in Howick and Hastings in New Zealand; Quinto's on Charing Cross Road in London; Elliot Bay in Seattle; and the awesome Strand in New York. The open-air used bookstalls in London on the South Bank nearly always have something I "need".

The used book has an intrinsic value all of its own. It doesn't have to be particularly beautiful or well kept if it appears to have a history, which many of them do. A signature inside of the cover is often a clue to its history. Often there are old bookmarks or notes in margins. Most are worth no more than what you pay for them but many are worth much more just for the pleasure of owning them.

As a matter of personal conviction I always shop independent stores wherever I can and for whatever I want. That's because I don't like any large business that squeezes the little guy out whether he or she be a butcher, baker, candlestick maker, or small book vendor. One reason is that I quickly get to know the owner and staff and can seek their advice or, as sometimes happens, I can bring them up-to-date on books of my genre of choice. I recall with great pleasure the late Bill Duthie's on Robson at Hornby in downtown Vancouver with his store for remainders a few blocks west. Sadly, they, and the one on 4th Ave, have fallen to the despicable cannibals.

Small bookstores feel good and look good. They have lots of places to sit down. Big stores fear that people sitting don't buy—smaller ones know that a customer must browse. He wants to feel the texture and if it's a used book, see who used to own it and when—and speculate why he parted with it. A former used bookstore owner tells me that most of his books came from browsing through estates and that for him was the most fun of what he did. (If you want to see my kind on the silver screen, get *84 Charing Cross Road* with Anne Bancroft, Anthony Hopkins, and Judith Dench—a simply marvellous movie just for the book lover.)

The proprietor of 32 Books talks about her place in the community, her dealing with charities, and bringing authors in for chats with customers. She expects those who work with her to read the latest books so they can knowingly converse with customers. The owner of the used bookstore knows his books. You may get a bargain but rarely a "deal". I must confess that of the hundreds of used books I've bought, only once have I bought a rare book at a cheap rate, my only "victory" being a Roderick Haig-Brown first edition for $10NZ in Auckland.

There is, of course, an element of surprise at smaller stores; you see a book you've forgotten or perhaps just a book that somehow didn't do anything for you when you first saw it but now calls out to you. I love to simply browse but I'm a bookaholic who rarely leaves without what I feel are damned good reads under my arm.

Customers in small bookstores are nicer than in the giant stores—or they certainly seem that way. My favourite stores are fun to be in—such as the ones I know in Staffa and Mull (Inner

Hebrides), Stromness (Orkney), and Budapest where with only fifty or so English language books, I managed to buy two!

Recently, Wendy asked if I would drop by 32 Books, who were holding a book for her. "This doesn't mean you must buy a book just because you're there," she said.

And I didn't. I bought two!

Will the new digital age be the death knell of the small bookstore? It'll be tough. Small stores must make many adjustments and even carry e-books themselves. They must fund innovative yet inexpensive ways to advertise their wares. It's tough now and will get a hell of a lot tougher but small shops have something Indigo Chapters doesn't have—a deep love for books and for people that want them, in places where you might just find a Labrador retriever casing the new selections or asleep in one of the armchairs as in 32 Books.

Let me add this postscript: there are many small bookstores and used bookstores near you. Small town BC always has a "real" bookstore and it'll survive if you help it. It'll make both you and the proprietor much happier than either of you were before you came in.

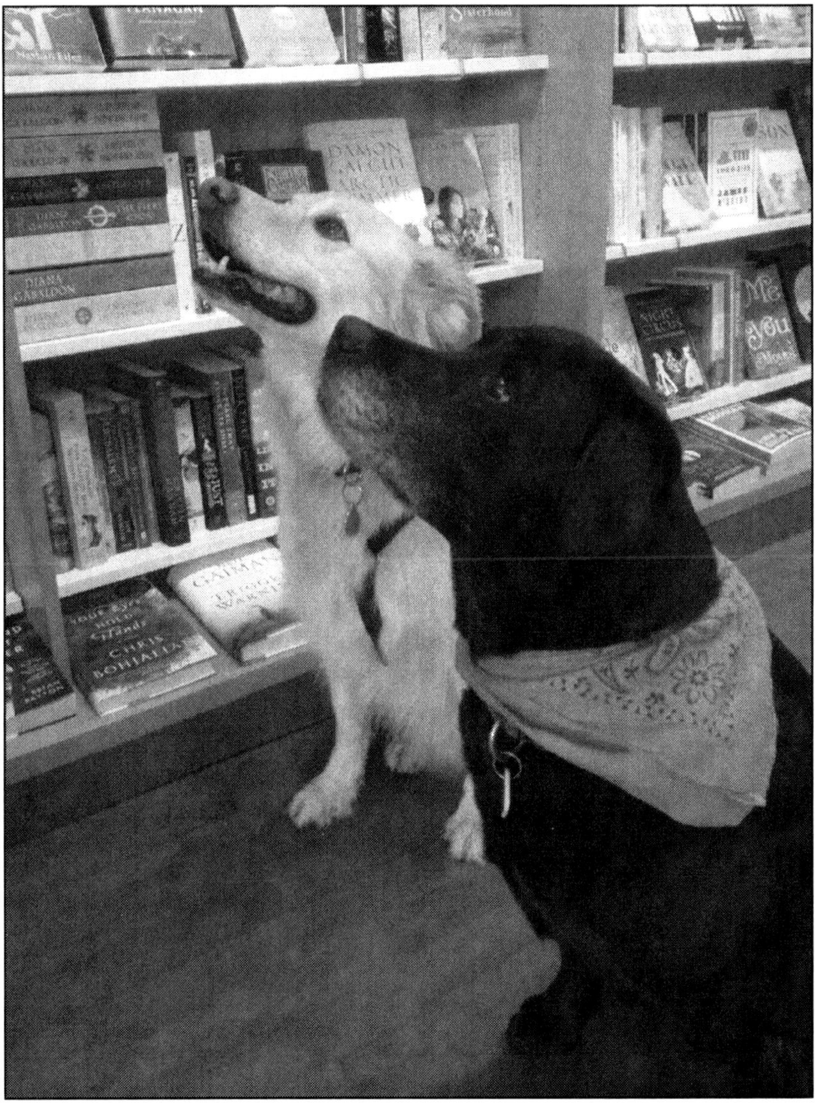

Two Canine Customers.

32 Books in Edgemont, West Vancouver, where both the books and browsers have class.

THE ELECTRONIC BOOK ARRIVES

Maybe eBooks are going to take over, one day, but not until those whizz kids in Silicon Valley invent a way to bend the corners, fold the spine, yellow the pages, add a coffee ring or two and allow the plastic tablet to fall open at a favourite page.
– Russell T. Davies

Will Wendy and I ever get e-books?

In fact, we bought each other Kindles for Christmas five years ago and it happened like this: on a September 2010 flight to Britain to start a three-week cruise, we flew a "charter" airline and were nailed nearly $600 as a penalty because our bags, carrying several books each, were too heavy! (On the way home we weren't, mercifully, nailed by Air Canada.) We'd have been better off to throw the books away and buy them again when we got home! It's hard to resist an e-book on monetary terms when you travel a lot.

For our cruise in the Caribbean in December 2011, to celebrate my eightieth, we loaded up our new kindles. I must say I was impressed at the tiny cost involved—many Classics are free. Even new books are much less than the printed version. What truly impressed me was that I could increase the font, an important consideration for aging eyes. The verdict was that we loved our e-books, especially for travel.

I find my Kindle very useful for storing up books without occupying shelf space, which I suppose is the whole idea. I have a bunch of baseball books that I got very cheap—in the $5 range—which I often read at bed time when I've had enough of the serious book for a bit. As an example, my main read at this writing is a biography of the great US jurist and revolutionary, John Marshall, but last night I took a break and picked up where I had left off with a biography of Shoeless Joe Jackson.

But for all its virtues, the e-book is not a book! It doesn't look like a book or feel like a book but I wonder, sadly, if anyone will care in a year or two. I believe that some always will and publishers will recognize this.

MY ENVIRONMENTALISM

Why are ecologists and environmentalists so feared and hated? This is because in part what they have to say is new to the general public, and the new is always alarming.

– Garrett Hardin

Thank God men cannot fly, and lay waste the sky as well as the earth.

– Henry David Thoreau

In addition to our attitude toward First Nations, there has been another huge change during my lifetime and it has been a very subtle one. Slowly, very slowly the public is forcing government and industry toward the "Precautionary Principle", namely "*if an action or policy has a suspected risk of causing harm to the public or to the environment, in the absence of scientific consensus that the action or policy is not harmful, the burden of proof that it is not harmful falls on those who advocate taking the action.*"

Not long ago, Premier Christy Clark, after the Lake Polley mine disaster, flew over the lake and made the idiotic statement that she would make it pretty again. But just as I thought she was slowly, very slowly, catching on to the fact that the public will no longer stand for environmental destruction and British Columbia has long been in the vanguard of change, she demonstrated that, like the Bourbons, she has learned nothing and forgotten nothing as she has uncritically embraced the LNG industry. One need only note the rather pallid opposition of Ontario thus far to the building of the eastern pipeline and compare that to the outrage in BC over the proposed Enbridge line and Kinder Morgan expansion for demonstrable proof that Clark and her Fraser Institute acolytes in cabinet are heading for a big time collision with the people.

In fact, "environmentalism" has become a major worldwide force. For most of my life, industry has been able to move in and tote up the value of the area in terms of timber, minerals, and so on, and the value for the beauty of the area was not part of the equation. We never thought we could quantify a beautiful mountain, lovely lake, or a gorgeous ocean shore. Those things were there, they were ours, but they had no monetary value; consequently, we simply accepted the fact that they would be impaired or destroyed. We didn't like it, but we had no choice. Governments, then and lamentably still, also accepted this and industry had a free ride and still does.

That has slowly but most surely changed. Wendy and I live on Howe Sound and along with our neighbours are appalled at the consequences of an LNG plant in Squamish or a gravel operation going into the mouth of McNab Creek. It's not just the traditional concerns that are being expressed. It's the aesthetic values as well that are front and centre and being expressed in strong terms. This manifested itself in the 2014 municipal election when an outsider, opposed to an LNG plant in Squamish, thumped the incumbent mayor of Squamish who was for it. She is now supported by a majority of her Council and the "David and Goliath" battle is on.

Companies don't understand this surge of environmentalism nor do the governments that they run. If you were to speak to somebody like the big mouth easterner, Joe Oliver, Minister of Finance, who's always flapping on about how BC must accept these desecrations, you see an indifference to such things as the beautiful mountains, lovely oceans, lakes, and so on. That simply does not compute in the minds of people like Oliver nor the prime minister. Nor yet, indeed, for the BC Premier, Christy Clark, who sees most everything in terms of money only. They remind me of Oscar Wilde's definition of a cynic as "knowing the cost of everything and the value of nothing," These non-monetary matters are just not factors to be considered.

It's much different with the people, and changing every day. Enbridge and Kinder Morgan, each seeking pipeline concessions in BC, are stunned at the attitude of people toward their trees and the rivers, as are corporations in general, putting them ahead of "progress". They and their client governments will have to change because people have changed and insist that their views be recognized.

People evolve. British Columbians have altered their views on questions of aboriginal peoples and the quantifying of our beautiful surroundings, which, just as timber and minerals, have a value. Those attitudinal changes are permanent and governments and industries are going to have to adjust to that.

My environmentalism comes naturally as it does to most British Columbians. For First Nations, it's bred into the soul. People from other parts of Canada can't understand our opposition to pipelines and LNG facilities and things of that nature; to oppose tanker traffic on our coast seems to be certifiable lunacy—isn't shipping one of our main businesses? (The answer happens to be no if you're talking bitumen or LNG.) It should be noted that when Americans were going to ship LNG up the East Coast, Prime Minister Harper set his hair on fire and it was banned! Apparently the East Coast of Canada is easier to see from Ottawa than is the West Coast.

British Columbians are simply not understood by the government of Canada and it's not likely they ever will be. The possible saving grace is the eastern pipeline and it may well be that environmentalism strikes Ontario, which will make it a national issue.

The question often arises as to my politics—blue, bluish, pinkish, or red? Does it matter? The answer is not philosophical but "environmental"—I'm a product of feelings, not deep philosophical thinking. To many, where they live is secondary to what they do. Not so with me!

In 1984, I was offered a safe seat in Parliament. I was rushed hard but I never hesitated. I would not, under any circumstances, move to Ottawa. In 1956, after law school, I took a job in Edmonton and within a few weeks was so homesick and broke, with a wife and baby and no job, that I came home. I'm not proud of this trait and admire the flexible. It's simply the way I am. A long way of saying that my politics and my lifelong love of British Columbia and Vancouver are the same.

Left or right, Mair, spit it out, man! Leftie?

I can only cite my record and let you decide.

As Environment Minister in a right wing Social Credit government, I stopped the government poisoning wolves, put a moratorium on the exploration for and mining of uranium, and saved the lovely Skagit River from being made into a huge lake by Seattle Light and Power by raising the High Ross Dam, something they were entitled to do under a 1941 agreement with the BC government. On the last, many caucus members thought that I was nuts giving up a new lake with all those expensive homes, speedboats, etc.

This was my record in a "right wing" government. Now, operating from precisely the same philosophy, I take the same environmental stances yet now I'm a "left winger"! Surely these designations are badly out-dated. What we face today is the corporatization of our lives with governments being unwilling to hold back the predations of their corporate friends—their paymasters. Environmental protection laws are a disgrace with the public denied a real voice in environmental protection commissions like the National Energy Board, shams that do the developers' bidding.

Some obvious examples of corporations trumping the public

interest can be found with fish farms, desecration of farmland for highways and development; proposed pipelines and oil tankers on our coast, fracking, LNG plants, trashing our rivers to make energy we can't use, destroying BC Hydro in the bargain and much more, all as payoffs to large corporations for political support.

Postscript: our new environmental consciousness has led to a new household duty ...

THE GARBAGE DETAIL

More than at any time in history mankind faces a crossroads. One path leads to despair and utter hopelessness, the other to total extinction. Let us pray that we have the wisdom to choose correctly.
– Woody Allen

Always do right; this will gratify some people and astonish the rest.
– Mark Twain

Like most households, we have a division of labour at our place. I do the writing, the broadcasting, the speechmaking, and the garbage, with the last requiring as much mental effort as the others combined.

We live in a townhouse and the garbage bins are about 200 metres away through a parking lot with two speed bumps. I'm not sure if the bumps slow cars down but they sure as hell call for careful moves for a wheelbarrow full to overflowing with garbage, pushed by a man with terrible knees. I'll try almost any combination of things, not necessarily wise, to avoid taking two trips! I consider it a perfect day if I negotiate these perils without having papers fall or plastic bottles roll down the lot. I often draw a bit of a crowd for this weekly adventure. The decisions to be made would be awesome if life depended on the outcome, but still, if one takes the duty seriously, one must apply the brain to the task.

I must confess a sin from the outset. Because I'm partly disabled, Wendy brings the big bag down from the kitchen. My problem is horrid knees, which my orthopaedic surgeon says means that, according to the X-rays, I can't walk. Bad squash too late in life. So, when the big plastic bag arrives, I cheat and throw all the contents of my waste paper basket into it and, here it comes, folks, often with orange peels, used ballpoint pens, a plastic water bottle, and all my waste paper. I wonder if someone at the business end of all that garbage is launching an investigation into who is so egregiously breaking the rules? Is it a jailing offence, I wonder?

When I get to the bins, the decisions begin. If I throw the big plastic bag into the main bin, should I be dumping the garbage in, then putting the plastic bag in the plastics bin? Or just toss the lot in? The hell with it—I throw the lot in the big bin and thus disappears the original sin into anonymity—I hope!

Then I get to those little plastic containers berries come in—you know the sort, flimsy plastic with the berries held in by cellophane—and I have a decision to make. Certainly these things are plastic but aren't they also cleaned containers? Eenie meeny miny mo—into the clean containers bin with you.

Then come the newspapers and one-ply cardboard bin. I assume that beer cases are one-ply cardboard except I notice some of my neighbours tossing them into the general bin. Maybe I should snitch on them and let the Garbage Czar make a ruling on them, not me. Bugger it; I put them with the papers but what to do with egg containers? They don't look much like paper to me and they don't feel like plastic—I opt for the big bin.

Then I come to the puzzler—the coffee can, which is a metal container with a plastic top. If I throw the top in the plastics does the rest still count as a container? I say to hell with it, it's *all* a container.

Then it's the plastic bottles. My boss doesn't wash these out so they're not "clean" containers but I pronounce them clean anyway, and into the plastics they go.

What about the orange juice container? As far as I can determine, it's paper with a plastic coating. It's a container too but somehow I don't think the garbage experts think of it that way, so is it paper or plastic? Piss on it, it's into the main bin.

Now it's the little tin cans that held the smoked oysters Wendy and I love at cocktail time. This brings the whole matter of containers to the fore once again. When they made the rules about containers, did they mean only containers that could be reused? If so, the smoked oyster container is no longer a container—again, when in doubt, use the big bin.

Usually I just act in accordance with the rules I have established but sometimes waiting and watching is a neighbour who acts as if he knows about these things and could report you. It's sort of like someone reading over your shoulder, but worse. This neighbour expresses his opinion by grunts and sotto voce mutterings as to where he or she—this is a husband and wife team we're talking about here, sometimes one, other times the other—would have put that plastic bottle with the metallic top invariably followed by a bit of a lecture, not directed at me, you understand, just to the world in general about the heavy burden the garbage detail involves and the importance of doing it right.

I go home with an empty wheelbarrow and a mind full of guilt that lasts until the next week.

OH THE DAYS DWINDLE DOWN TO A PRECIOUS FEW

Oh when I was young and easy
In the mercy of its means
Time held me green and dying
Though I sang in my chains like the sea.
– Dylan Thomas, Welsh poet

Growing old is not for the faint of heart.

Much of life is denial, of course, and a slightly buried feeling of contemptuous pity of those going or gone. Maybe it's an inner feeling that when our time comes, science will have found a cure for death. We never pause to consider what to do with all the people of course!

I have undertaken some important steps to avoid death:

I'll never be a stunt man for the movies.

Climbing cliff faces or any sort of work in high places is not on—constructing tall buildings and bridges I cheerfully leave to the Mohawks, I will not be playing Russian Roulette, and I'll not be a volunteer to defuse bombs and land-mines. I won't be the stooge for the knife thrower at the Midway—speaking of Midways, I'll not die on a roller coaster or any other similar contrivance.

I'll not be fighting bullies in bars and I won't be eating that Japanese fish, which, if it isn't cooked properly, brings instant death.

I won't be skiing in bounds much less out of bounds and jumping is quite out of the question as is, of course, bobsledding, now that I know from our Winter Olympics what a "luge" is!

Car racing is out—so is motorcycle racing. No motorcycles, period. (Speaking of motorcycles, when I see the woman driving and the man sitting behind holding on for dear life, I will know that the battle of the sexes is over.)

I won't be scuba diving or doing any other kind of water games that are over my head. I won't die from standing up in a canoe—or sitting down in one, for that matter, or certainly not making love in one!

I won't be falling off any roofs or other high places, I'll not have a heart attack climbing the Grouse Grind or similar foolishness, and I'll not die defending myself with a weapon against a burglar.

I won't die from being on a suspension bridge that collapses. When I was a boy I used swing on a rope over the most dangerous spot in Lynn Creek—there will not be any replays.

I won't be killed by a crazed hitchhiker or any other kind, come to think of it, and I'll not be trapped in any cave or coal mine.

I won't die bungee jumping, parachuting with or without a parachute, diving off tall cliffs, hang-gliding, flying in ultra light planes, parasailing, tight-rope walking, high diving, or standing on the wings of a barnstorming biplane. I'm aided in this resolve by an extraordinary fear of heights.

One of my grandsons ran with the bulls at Pamplona—I will not be doing the same. Similarly, I'll not die as a picador, much less the matador, at the Bull Fights.

I will not die holding a tropical snake, or spider, or the tsetse fly—much less a rampaging hungry beast of the tropics; nor will I swim where there are crocodiles or Piranha fish. I won't be swallowed in quicksand as I nearly was. (I digress to tell you of a *New Yorker* cartoon showing two explorers in quicksand up to their necks and one says to the other, "I'm tempted to struggle!") It goes without saying that I won't be wrestling crocodiles or bears.

As a positive step in the psychology part of avoiding death, Wendy and I impose the ten-minute rule on unhappy conversations—we have ten minutes before the gong to discuss sickness in whatever form to anyone, deaths, families, or any other soft of ongoing grief.

Ah, but is that enough?

Somehow I doubt it and the Grim Reaper will find me in due course.

AU REVOIR

Optimism is the faith that leads to achievement. Nothing can be done without hope and confidence.
– Helen Keller, the first deaf and blind person to earn a Bachelor of Arts degree.

What does the future hold?

It is very hard to be optimistic when one looks at what we're doing to the world in general. I'm not going to comment on the effects of global warming, not because I don't believe it is a serious problem—it is—but because I simply cannot predict what will happen if matters carry on as they are. I do believe there are reasons for some optimism. Mankind has a history of only facing things when they become desperate. The question here, of course, is have things gotten too desperate to do anything about them? That I'll have to leave for a future I will not live to see.

My optimism comes from the people of British Columbia

themselves. It's always a danger that newcomers won't see the problems as those of us who have lived here a long time see them. However, again to be optimistic, newcomers tend to be enchanted by what they see and very often become like converts to a religion. Many people come here because of the beauties of the place and want to preserve those beauties once when they get here.

As I write this there is a strong environmental movement within the province. That doesn't prevail in equal measure everywhere in the province, of course. However, it is to be noted that in the Peace River area, the principal provider of fossil fuels, a large portion of the public has risen to fight Site "C" and the devastation it will wreak on the area despite the promised jobs and general prosperity.

There is also, in my view, a healthy cynicism about what our leaders, industrial and political, tell us. No longer do we simply accept the word of either of these two groups as to what the consequences of their planned action will be. In times past, opposition came from the gut, not the brain; however, it is now from both. Environmentalists are far better informed if only because so many scientists have become involved.

I am, therefore, reasonably confident that British Columbia will fight like hell to preserve itself. This will not come easily, of course. One only need look at the Sunshine Coast to see where developers are slavering to build things and bring people into the area. Some of this is bound to happen. One of the great pluses of this area, however, might be seen as a negative—it does not have very many sandy beaches. With the exception of the Sechelt Inlet, most of the beaches are small stone, quite suitable for swimming and sunbathing but not the sort of beaches that bring people from thousands of miles away to enjoy. Much, of course, will depend upon local authorities and how strong they can be.

I am cautiously optimistic because having spent my life in BC, I think I know the people. They have a special love for their province and are willing to fight both industry and government to protect it.

I think the best thought for those going through life, trying their best to cope, comes from the great Scottish Bard, Sir Harry Lauder, whose words comforted Churchill during World War II:

"Keep right on to the end of the road, keep right on to the end,

Tho' the way be long, let your heart be strong, keep right on round the bend.

Tho' you're tired and weary still journey on, till you come to your happy abode,

Where all you love you've been dreaming of will be there at the end of the road."

I want to close very briefly with these two thoughts about the very best and the very worst of the great town I grew up in.

The worst first: every summer there was an epidemic of infantile paralysis or more commonly called polio. It scared the hell out of the entire community and each year the toll included at least someone you knew. Until the Salk vaccine was invented in the '50s, this terror was always with us.

The second is the best: this was the autumn when the chestnuts came out and conkers began. Conkers, of course, are chestnuts with a string through them and the idea is to take turns challenging someone else with a conker to a duel, each trying to smash the other's. This is an art form that not only calls for getting a nice big juicy chestnut, but also soaking it in linseed oil and caring for it as if it were a child. Every year we would try to rush the season and take chestnuts off the tree when they weren't ready. Every year this failed for one really had to wait until the chestnuts hit the ground and then scavenge to get the very best one.

This time of year, with the smell of chestnut trees, the arrival of the conkers and the lovely general sense of autumn in the air was the very best moment in the "city of the horse buns", except when the cherry blossoms come out on the Stanley Park Causeway, early in February, and those eastern bastards eat their hearts out!

ABOUT THE AUTHOR

Rafe Mair is a best-selling Canadian author with nine published works including *Canada, Is Anyone Listening?* and *Radio Daze*. A lawyer by trade, Rafe was elected to the British Columbia legislature in 1975 and served as a Cabinet Minister under Premier Bill Bennett until 1980, when he retired from politics and reinvented himself as a radio talk-show host. Brash, opinionated and (usually) well-informed, Rafe dominated the West Coast airwaves for twenty-five years, championing social justice and environmentalism. Today he makes his home just north of Vancouver, BC, with his beloved wife Wendy.